D1242189

The Power of Adversity is a courageous book in which legendary businessman and philanthropist Al Weatherhead describes how adversity—properly understood—can be a catalyst for powerful and meaningful personal transformation. Read it and be inspired—for yourself and for someone you love. Highly recommended.

—Dean Ornish, MD
Founder and President,
Preventive Medicine Research Institute
Clinical Professor of Medicine,
University of California, San Francisco
Author, The Spectrum and Dr. Dean Ornish's
Program for Reversing Heart Disease

THE
POWER OF
ADVERSITY

Tough Times Can Make You Stronger, Wiser, and Better

AL WEATHERHEAD WITH FRED FELDMAN

for the evolving human spirit

HAMPTON ROADS
PUBLISHING COMPANY, INC.

Cover design by Steve Amarillo

Hampton Roads Publishing Company, Inc.
1125 Stoney Ridge Road
Charlottesville, VA 22902

434-296-2772
fax: 434-296-5096
e-mail: hrpc@hrpub.com
www.hrpub.com

If you are unable to order this book from your local
bookseller, you may order directly from the publisher.
Call 1-800-766-8009, toll-free.

Library of Congress Cataloging-in-Publication Data
Weatherhead, Al, 1925-
  The power of adversity : tough times can make you stronger, wiser,
and better / Al Weatherhead, with Fred Feldman.
    p. cm.
  Summary: "Presents a different take on adversity: rather than suc-
cumbing to life's obstacles, we can use them to strengthen and improve
ourselves"--Provided by publisher.
  Includes bibliographical references and index.
  ISBN 978-1-57174-562-0 (5 x 7.25 tc : alk. paper)
 1. Success--Psychological aspects. 2. Self-management (Psychology)
3. Crisis management. 4. Suffering. 5. Self-actualization (Psychology)
I. Feldman, Fred, 1950- II. Title.
  BF637.S8W3375 2008
                    2007039737

             ISBN 978-1-57174-562-0
             10 9 8 7 6 5 4 3 2 1

        Printed on acid-free paper in the United States

What wee gave, wee have;
What wee spent, wee had;
What wee left, wee lost.

—*Edward Courtenay, Earl of Devon (1419)*

For
Celia

Contents

Foreword

by K. Lance Gould, MD

Our lives and histories are commonly altered by some catastrophe, bad luck, hardship, misfortune, or disaster, sometimes of our own doing and sometimes out of the blue. What's poison to one may be food for another, depending on one's point of view. In the gloom of some current trouble, we also dream of a happy ending, of getting through, of changing, getting around, or overcoming the difficulty. However, for some that dream dies with no happy ending. Adversity then imposes a choice of what we do with it.

Stories from the first cave paintings to Shakespeare to this weekend's movie recount these choices and their outcomes. In keeping with this tradition, this book recounts Al Weatherhead's life, arguing that adversity may be a source of power, power to a happy ending though perhaps not the one originally or conventionally imagined. We normal mortals connect with the great rags-to-riches, life-and-death stories through the flaws of the heroes. Their faults inspire us to believe we can overcome adversity, just as they did, despite our deficiencies or self-destructive traits.

Al had the genes and family environment to make or mess up his life, doing both in substantial portions. His story includes familial affection, conflict and rejection, an adventurous, hell-raising youth, discovering work and self, failure and success, debilitating pain, alcoholism, heart disease, and altruism. Here is everyman's antihero, with lots of knobs and bumps going somewhere in unexpected zigs and zags.

In most accounts of a man's adversity, a woman makes the story possible, as Celia Weatherhead does in this one. Without her, there would likely be no transcending the bad to the good, no story, only a number down. Al makes clear the essential role of a loving and loved woman in his story.

Adversity—coronary heart disease—brought Al to me. Constantly ahead of conventional thinking, he wanted a proactive alternative to bypass surgery, disability, or premature death. With characteristic intensity, he succeeded admirably with healthy food, hard workouts, and appropriate medications, resulting in improved blood flow through his coronary arteries by an advanced imaging technology called positron emission tomography, or PET, which I had been developing for the heart.

He also tested me with a modest research grant that

worked and then tested the entire University of Texas system with his innovative ideas on charitable funding. The adversities that he overcame in business and health bloomed into innovation given back in those same troubled areas of his life.

Philosophy/introspection and action/pragmatism are commonly opposing extremes. Rarely, all come together in one piece or one person. Al is the real thing. He has wrestled with his demons, walked the walk of life through thorns and roses, with Celia, and now gives back to the lives of others.

How to bounce back? The book tells you. It is a fascinating biography and an inspiring instruction manual for turning life's adversities to the good.

K. Lance Gould, MD

Acknowledgments

A decade ago I believed writing a book was as easy as rolling off a log. You sat down, wrote, and then your book was published. Now I know differently. A million words must be written before one is published.

My wife, Celia, is my guardian, guide, and stay. Her love and support throughout our lives is inestimable. Exposing my heart and soul to the world is gut wrenching and not easily done. She helped me ford the river of my adversity to the far bank and gave me life's precious gift: to know thyself. Thanks, Celia.

My deepest thanks and admiration to Rob Wilkens. Rob, you nurtured me through the early years; you were demanding, dedicated, and inspirational in telling me, "This story must be told."

Betsy Radin, you're a treasure. Thanks for your help and endless iterations. They were a blessing.

Fred Feldman, your good-natured poking and prodding were terrific and terrorizing. You never let me off the hook. Thank you.

As agent, friend, and guide, Al Zuckerman is the exemplar for all to follow.

At Hampton Roads, my greatest appreciation and gratitude to Jack Jennings and his hands-on group who were invaluable in their efforts in crafting this book.

A final thank you to all who have helped me in my life. You have all been wondrous, and I owe everything to your kindnesses.

ONE

We're Not Meant to Be Happy . . . We're Meant to Grow

> When written in Chinese the word "crisis" is composed of two characters—one represents danger and the other represents opportunity.
>
> —*John F. Kennedy*

We face adversity every day. We spend most of our lives trying to bounce back from it. I'm not talking about gremlinlike, daily irritations such as traffic jams, computer glitches, and so on. We can usually shrug those off pretty well. I'm referring to tragic, life-changing adversity like cancer, divorce, and getting fired.

Such major adversity can drive any of us to contemplate the unthinkable: committing suicide quickly with a gun, a razor blade, or an overdose of pills, or killing ourselves more slowly, but just as effectively, by drowning our pain in booze or obliterating it, along with our minds, with mood-altering, addictive drugs.

Major adversity more often than not is the culprit that brings about the so-called deaths by natural causes of heart attack and stroke. And then there are the accidental deaths stemming from automobile accidents, plane crashes, and the various other tragedies attributed to human error or unknown mechanical failures. Nor can we rule out personal adversity and its role in distracting us and affecting our judgment at critical moments, from the pilot landing an airplane, to the mechanic servicing brakes, to the stressed-out mom or dad behind the wheel of the family car running a red light or not seeing a stop sign.

In all these dismal scenarios adversity breaks down our bodies and taxes our spirits with overwhelming despair. It is the Pandora's Box that floods us with misery. But there can be another scenario, if we learn how to tame adversity and make it *serve* us.

Believe me, I know, because I've had my share of major adversity, and from an early age.

I was born the son of an alcoholic and grandson of an alcoholic. I grew up and became an alcoholic, too.

I can only guess that my father abused alcohol to escape from huge self-induced stress due to his Type-A personality and his work as an industrialist. I often saw my father have beer at breakfast, drink whiskey at noon, and sleep until dinner. And here is the hardest part for me to tell you: *I welcomed his drunkenness.* Why? When he was sober, my father was cold and aloof. The only time my father ever told me "I love you" was when he was drunk.

I began sneaking drinks when I was twelve. My father was fun, affectionate, and warm when he was drunk. I wanted to be those things, too. At one point in my life as a drunkard, I could get from my bedroom to the basement, remove the hinge pins from the locked liquor cabinet, make a very dry twenty-ounce martini, replace the door, fly up the stairs, pausing at the kitchen fridge to throw ice in my oversized glass, and be back in my bedroom in less than ninety seconds. In this way I could drink to my heart's content while the household slept.

Later in this book I will tell more about how my drinking almost destroyed me. For now, I'll just make the point that my experience with adversity has not been limited to alcoholism. Far from it.

In My Life . . .

- Just graduated from Harvard, bitter and frustrated over a falling-out with my father concerning my place in the family business, I hopped from one dead-end job to another. In

Houston, I was a roustabout for Eastern States Petroleum; in Stamford, Connecticut, I was a stock chaser at Yale & Towne Manufacturing Company. I quit that job to move to Pittsburgh to do menial work in a factory that made road-paving equipment. I pretended I was finding myself, but in truth, my tumbleweed, professional odyssey was symptomatic of my utter inability to cope with the adversity of my dashed hopes and expectations concerning my working alongside my father.

- On a cruelly beautiful spring day in Connecticut, I had the heart-rending experience of burying my firstborn infant son. I stood trembling, the tears streaming down my cheeks, barely hearing the minister as I felt my own heart and soul sinking with my baby boy's tiny casket into that cold, dark grave.

- I tore through two marriages in a frenzy of shouted accusations, slammed doors, and lengthy, bitter court battles, and almost ruined my third union with the woman who was and is my soul mate.

- I severed all ties with my father over our dispute about my place in the family business, a schism that sent me on week-long drunken binges in squalid flop houses.

- I suffered the terrors of clinical depression, crippling arthritis, and heart disease.

Eventually I came to see these adversities for what they were: blessings in disguise that I learned to leverage to make me a stronger, wiser, more loving, and more creative human being.

Today, I am a recovering alcoholic. I am the proud father of three children, grown into happy, productive adults. I'm deeply in love with my wife, and I'm happy to say that I reconciled with my father before his death. I also conquered both my depression and my arthritis, and my body now shows no physical evidence of heart disease.

In addition, I've been able to build a multimillion-dollar manufacturing company that provided me with the means to be a major philanthropist, endowing hospitals, universities, and charities that offer valuable help to thousands of people.

I tell you this not to brag, but to make the point that I had sunk as low as I thought one could go. Then things turned around for me.

So how did I manage to bounce back from a hellish pit of adversity when my younger brothers, David and Dick, experiencing many of the same tribulations, were unable to tame their addictions and succumbed far too early to their physical illnesses? Why am I now here, writing about mastering the power of adversity, when

David literally drank himself to death in a lonely apartment? (I can see him now as I saw him on his last days, sprawled in the dark in his oversized chair, drinking endless Seagram's Sevens, smoke from his pipe swirling about his head as he vainly attempted to soothe his torments by listening to Strauss waltzes.)

These questions both tormented and fascinated me. I forced myself to look inward, observing myself, trying to pinpoint what had allowed me to persevere and succeed. I quizzed myself: *What was I doing now in my life that I wasn't doing when adversity was threatening to overwhelm me? How had I changed?*

My introspection provided me with a sudden illumination. I realized that I had at some point recognized serious adversity for what it is: the natural order of life. Adversity is meant to act like a grain of sand inside an oyster; it is the irritant in our lives that can stimulate us to create pearls. In short, I came to understand the power of adversity and some of the lessons it can teach us, starting with the all-important truth in this chapter's title:

WE ARE NOT MEANT, IN THE GRAND SCHEME OF LIFE, TO BE HAPPY AND COMFORTABLE. RATHER, WE ARE MEANT TO FORGE OUR CHARACTERS ON THE ANVIL OF ADVERSITY.

Since then, I've been formulating the premises of this book. I've come to believe most of us experience monumental periods of adversity—perfectly timed and honed—to burn away our self-deception. These devastating setbacks propel us in our quest to become fully and creatively human. Sometimes we get stuck, so stuck, in fact, that only great pain will impel us to move. It's then that the power of adversity is revealed. But to see it requires a new way of looking at the world, a radical shifting of perspective.

In this book, I propose that you learn to look at your life, what happens to you, and what you do, in a different way. A lot of what I have to tell you has been cryptically condensed into folk sayings that have come to us down through the ages. Trouble is, we've all heard that stuff so many times we take it for granted or, even worse, dismiss it as nothing but hoary old clichés. For example, how often have you heard the following?

- Think positively.
- Every cloud has a silver lining.
- Whatever doesn't kill you makes you stronger.
- You have to learn the hard way.
- Every challenge is an opportunity.

The invaluable secret at the core of these folk wisdoms is that our lives are journeys of transformation, and each time the catalyst for change is painful circumstances. We can't grow as human beings without seeing ourselves—and our relationships to others—through the unique and challenging lens of adversity.

Most of us at some level know this deep inside ourselves. We value this truth in our entertainments, for instance. We thrill to novels, movies, TV shows, and plays in which characters face confrontation, often just another word for adversity. From *Gone with the Wind* to *Star Wars,* we feel the emotional charge, empathy, and truth when we watch initially shallow individuals who, facing adversity, must rise to the occasion (often at great personal cost), and come through their ordeal having learned lessons that make them stronger, kinder, wiser—*better*—than before.

In our own lives, however, many of us do not rise to these challenges of adversity. Instead, we accept these failings, telling ourselves we deserved them or there's nothing we can do about them. But this is a huge mistake. More to the point, it is a terrible and tragic *waste* not to seize adversity to use to your advantage.

Adversity taught me that my seemingly most terrible moments—from professional catastrophes to the soul-shattering experience of losing a child—were actually only part of a lifelong process of maturing. I am today convinced that I was being prepared by adversity to do what was necessary to become healthy, loving, and loved.

I don't mean to suggest that I at the time *welcomed* such adversity, or that my life is now perfect. Nobody wants trouble, and nobody has a perfect life. But thanks to adversity, I now have a different way of looking at life, which has revitalized me to the point that at eighty plus years, I'm as active as many individuals half my age. Again, I'm not bragging, simply stating a fact.

My vigor does not stem from luck or heredity. As I have already said, my father was a periodic alcoholic. I was an alcoholic and am now, through AA, a recovering alcoholic. My father and my brother David died of cancer. My youngest brother, Dick, died of heart disease and alcoholism. I've battled physical and mental illnesses: alcoholism, crippling arthritis, heart disease, and clinical depression.

So what enabled me to recover? Adversity, which always brings with it the benefit of *learning the hard way* (to quote one of those old folk sayings). To tell the truth, I *can't* learn any other way. It was pure pain followed by hard learning that drove me away from my father and out on my own, keeping my nose to the grindstone in dead-end jobs. It was pure pain followed by hard learning that forced me to endure two miserable marriages before finding the love of my life. And, ultimately, if not for the hard learning bought and paid for by my excruciating arthritis, I might never have made it through my later, terrifying battle with heart disease.

As I look back, I now see that suffering, pain, and the threat of death were the only *hard lessons* strong enough to break through the thickness of my *hard head*. Like most, I used to think that disease, depression, and rejection were all life's enemies, and in a real and terrible sense that is true. Adversity is a double-edged sword that can crush the life and soul right out of a person. Yet, when you approach adversity humbly and creatively, it can set off a powerful and transforming chain reaction.

To put it another way: every *challenge* is an *opportunity*—the last folk saying I listed above—for us to grow. This is the incredible power of adversity, and it can be harnessed by each of us. I did it. You can do it, too.

This book provides helpful and pragmatic information on harnessing the power of adversity for yourself. I'll share exercises, tips, and advice that you can use to make adversity work for you instead of against you.

First, a caveat. This is not a book about God. In these pages I take no position on whether we are destined to suffer in some divine sense, whether such suffering and subsequent potential redemption is God's will, whether we are meant to endure terrible adversity on Earth as the dues we pay for a blissful afterlife, and so on.

My approach to the question of why adversity exists is entirely pragmatic. This is a *self-help* book. Remember my example about the grain of sand inside the oyster that turns into a pearl? That's scientific fact, not metaphor. It's my contention that, just like that grain of sand is used by the oyster, we can use adversity as a catalyst for creating something good—if we know how. To that end, I've devised a list of rules one can use to help put adversity to work:

THE RULES FOR MASTERING ADVERSITY

1. We're not meant to be happy . . . we're meant to grow.

2. Positive thinking is imperative.

3. You are not at the center of the universe.

4. Instead of "Why *me?* . . . Why *not* me?"

5. It is luckier to *earn* than to *receive.*

6. Be *self*-ish and put yourself *first,* by putting yourself *last.*

7. Never think "I *have* to do it." Instead, think "I have *it* to do."

8. I *suffer* passes . . . I *suffered* never passes . . . A blade remains tempered long after the fire that scorched it has faded away.

9. Cultivate the seven *self*-ish virtues of modesty, gratitude, courtesy, self-control, compassion, perseverance, and indomitable spirit to conquer your adversity.

10. Adversity creates walls . . . When you tear down those walls you create spectacular vistas of self-potential.

11. Leverage sweat equity built up by surviving previous trouble to help master current adversity.

12. Adversity always grants a chance to creatively resolve the problem.

13. Running away never helps.

14. Overcoming adversity requires the right attitude . . . meditation . . . communication . . . and sharing.

15. Have the right idea about money. Success isn't just possessions and power.

16. Practice responsibility, loyalty, consideration—the magic formula that is the secret to life.

17. Always get the facts . . . real facts, not the imagined ones.

18. Treat time as your most valuable resource.

19. Get perspective through acts of charity to others.

20. Adversity provides the only real opportunity to make an incredible difference in your life and in the world.

21. Come to see problem solving as one of the great joys of life.

22. There is always a great idea lurking in adversity . . . Will you find it?

As I expand on these rules in the pages to follow, I hope to inform and inspire you to see what's possible when you move through adversity to a greater understanding of life and its goodness.

Facing adversity is never easy. I'll do my best not to minimize the sheer terror and difficulty associated with suffering as I offer ways to use adversity to better ourselves and the world we share. I invite you to share my experiences, thoughts, hopes, and lessons, so you can move closer to the mystery, wonder, and power of life, by transforming your adversity into a force for positive change.

TWO

If I'm at the Center of the Universe . . . Where Are You?

Once the game is over, the king and the pawn go back into the same box.

—Unknown

In 1983, twelve years after starting my own company, two momentous things altered my life: an *invention* and an *affliction.* The invention produced a patent and fantastic sales growth. The affliction was a chronic disease that would leave me crippled and suffering, facing long odds for a comeback.

The invention convinced me I was at the center of the universe.

The affliction proved to me I was not.

The Invention

In 1971, with heavy financing and a tiny amount of cash, I purchased a small, two-customer plastics company in Twinsburg, Ohio. A new start, a new company, a new name: Weatherchem Corporation. We were on a roll; sales had leaped by tenfold and employment had trebled. It was substantial incremental growth, but it was not the success I had been counting on and dreaming of my entire life. What was slowing Weatherchem down? My company lacked revenue-generating *patents.*

Thomas Edison, the King of Invention, held more than eleven hundred patents. Growing up, I had made it my goal to have more patents than my father, who, through his company, acquired nearly seven hundred of them. (So far, I've not been able to surpass my father's record.) Yet, in 1983, it took just one patentable invention to launch my company into the stratosphere.

We called it the Weatherchem Flapper®.

In your kitchen you probably have a spice- or powder-filled container with a plastic top that has two tabs—one for pouring or spooning, and one for sprinkling. That top is most likely derived from the original Flapper my company invented in 1983.

Today there's an entire line of Flapper products used by over 150 companies, including McCormick, ACH Foods/Tones and Durkee, Kraft, Procter and Gamble, and Pharmative/Nature's Made. The Flapper has, in fact, become so common that it's taken for granted.

But it was not always that way. Although the idea for the Flapper was radically simple, its genesis was a complicated process. Like most patents, the Flapper came in response to a specific need. Durkee Spice Company came to Weatherchem asking if we might be able to develop a new plastic dispenser top with dual flaps. The idea was not a new one. Other companies had been working on similar concepts. But their caps leaked because the flaps popped open under the slightest pressure.

Durkee's challenge, then, came to me cloaked in a mantle of adversity: how could Weatherchem solve what other companies had concluded was an insurmountable problem?

Like most adversity, this *problem* was my *opportunity* to shine if my company could find the solution. I believed the invention of a new sprinkling and pouring cap held enormous potential for the growth and well-being of Weatherchem, because so many food companies might make use of such an innovative product.

So how could we engineer a product that poured and sprinkled but didn't leak? We went down many dead-end roads and endured long months of frustration trying to figure that out. We could have given up, like so many who had tried before us.

But we *didn't* give up, and finally mastered the adversity by devising a cap with flaps that didn't open and close on an inside hook like everyone else's caps did.

Instead, our cap's flaps opened and closed on a ridged outside perimeter that kept it from popping open and leaking.

We had our solution, but now we faced a second challenge. If we failed with our first Flapper mold we would be bankrupt. Remember, no one in the world was making such a product. While I was optimistic, I had no guarantee that, beyond Durkee, there would be interest in the device.

To go forward with the Flapper, or not? I was gambling my fledging company's future on a roll of the dice. A consensus from my Weatherchem team was not long in emerging: *"Hell, let's do it!"*

Later, after our initial success, we continued to spend vast sums to develop an entire family of Flapper products. The Flapper made Weatherchem a fortune. It truly changed my life.

Then again, so did my affliction.

The Affliction

Let me begin by saying that I was once a committed runner. One day in May 1983, when I was 58, I stood at the starting line of a 10-kilometer race. I was in peak condition. In addition to running, I had been swimming for decades, about 25 to 30 miles monthly—nearly 400 miles in the pool per year. This road race was merely a training exercise. I had been accepted to participate in the New York Marathon that fall, an experience that would fulfill one of my lifelong dreams.

The day of the 10K race was 40 degrees, with a light rain falling, the kind of damp, chilly weather that settles deep into your bones. I ran well enough, completing the race in 54 minutes, 37 seconds, and placing 3,332 among 10,000 participants. Not bad for a guy in his late 50s!

It was after the race that sudden cold swept through me, initially lasting only a few seconds at a time. Within days, however, spasms of chills and radiating back pain gripped me. At first I dismissed it as the typical aches and pains of a cold, but the condition intensified. The pain grew severe and migrated to different parts of my body: shoulders, knees, elbows, wrists, fingers, even my jaws. Eventually my condition was diagnosed as rheumatoid arthritis (RA).

Over the ensuing months my RA symptoms worsened, confining me to bed. By the beginning of 1984 my jaws ached so severely that all I could eat was baby food. My knees were so inflamed I was forced to use a walker. Beyond the physical pain, I was plunged into a morass of depression by the disease's devastating onslaught. And believe me, if anyone had dared to say to me then that this particular bout of adversity was a blessing in disguise, I would have punched him or her in the nose—assuming I could have lifted my arm.

My number for the upcoming New York Marathon

was X-146. What an honor to be chosen as one of the participants! Even during my darkest days I had kept the date—October 23—marked on my calendar. Somehow, someway, I continued to believe that I would run that race.

On October 14, my wife drove me to the post office. I couldn't drive. My neck was frozen stiff. Only the movement of my eyes allowed me to see left or right. My precious New York City Marathon number was placed in an envelope, sealed, and returned.

I can't begin to tell you how giving up my dream of participating in that marathon broke my heart. I also won't subject you to the details of my physical ordeal and the medical treatments in the months that followed. I will just say that I hurt so much that I was ready to die. I thought at the time, *Anything would be better than this . . .*

My first, positive step toward using the adversity of RA to improve myself came about by mere chance. As I learned more about RA, I was struck by the fact that one in five people recover completely from the disease. *One in five.* That fact became my mantra of *positive thinking.* I kept repeating it over and over. I knew that if I wasn't careful and failed to properly manage my mind, an unwanted echo would haunt me and undermine my determination: four out of five don't completely recover . . .

THIS IMPORTANT RULE
IN TERMS OF MANAGING ADVERSITY
BEARS REPEATING:
POSITIVE THINKING IS IMPERATIVE.

My positive thinking about my recovery changed my life and, in the process, gave my life back to me. You might say that my efforts to heal my *physical* self put me on the path to heal my *spirit.* However, getting there was an arduous journey for me. I had to lug an incredible amount of baggage along the way, mostly in the form of my long-festering rage toward my father.

My father, Albert J. Weatherhead Jr., was everything to me as I was growing up, but in retrospect, I think I knew even then that I could never please him. He was a Harvard graduate, a World War I flying ace who won a Silver Star for valor, an amateur boxing champion, and a football hero. In 1919, with less than a thousand dollars, he founded the Weatherhead Company, in the business of making and selling products for the control, containment, and transmission of fluid power. Within five decades, his company was listed as one of *Fortune's* top 500.

I desperately wanted to emulate my father and followed as closely as possible in his footsteps. Like him, I went to Harvard. I also served in the Army Air Corps during World War II (as a radio operator/mechanic, which was as close as I could get to being a fighter pilot, like he'd been). During all this time I dreamed of working alongside my father as heir-in-waiting to the presidency of the Weatherhead Company.

I'll never forget the day I entered my father's office with those regal visions dancing in my head, only to have the World War I flying ace promptly shoot me out of the sky. He told me that if I wanted to work for the family company I had to start as a lowly apprentice toolmaker in a subsidiary plant in the faraway town of Columbia City, Indiana, population five thousand.

I had nothing against starting at the bottom, but I had always assumed I would at least start at the bottom *as my father's apprentice,* interacting with him on a daily basis. I asked him how a blue-collar factory job in a desolate rural town would train me to someday take over the company and tried to negotiate a compromise position, but my father's offer was nonnegotiable.

In retrospect, I realize my father's tragic flaw: he was a real-life King Lear, a ruler who could not accept the fact that he would one day have to transfer his power and authority. That lowly job offer to me to be an apprentice toolmaker in some far-off subsidiary was merely a stalling tactic on his part.

My father probably didn't realize it (we are all so adept at self-delusion), but his tactic of exiling me was his attempt to deny the reality of the inevitable changing of the guard, symbolized by the daily ordeal of being forced to acknowledge his grown son coming to join him in the executive suite—even if all I wanted to do was sit at his feet so I could learn from him.

I turned my back on my father on that day. I told myself then that I was leaving him behind for good. But my anger and resentment stayed with me, ruining my professional prospects and personal relationships for years to come.

How can you leave anything behind when you are at the center of the universe?

Much later in my life, after the invention of the Weatherchem Flapper and in the midst of my struggles with RA, a good friend visited me. He began praising my father, saying he was a great man. I listened impatiently and finally exploded: "No! He cheated me out of my birthright!"

Perhaps for the first time in my life I heard myself give vent to my deep, raw, vengeful emotions. I immediately went into an internal dialog:

> Why do you hold your father in such low esteem?
> *Because he didn't give me what I wanted. What I was entitled to.*
> Why don't you—why can't you—get over it?
> *Because he never told me he was wrong or sorry!*
> Weren't those his problems, not yours?
> *No! Because he denied me what was rightfully mine!*
> Where has all this destructive self-importance and negative emotion brought you?

It's made me sick with arthritis after having steeped so long in my own poisons.

How did I come to that last conclusion? RA is classified formally as an autoimmune disease, which the *Mayo Clinic Family Health Book* defines as "a reaction of the body against one or some of its own tissues that are perceived as foreign substances, resulting in the production of antibodies against that tissue." In layperson's terms, my body, in one sense or another, had turned upon itself.

Later we'll explore the holistic nature of physical illnesses and how they relate to mental states. For now, suffice it to say that it took the adversity of RA to make me understand that this disease, in ways both literal and symbolic, was not just a matter of crippled joints and muscles, but of a constricting, crippling illness of emotions and spirit brought on in large part by my unresolved anger toward my father, which had closed me off from some of life's greatest experiences—most notably, placing trust in another person.

My stoic "break before bending" stance against the winds of adversity was my way of fulfilling my destiny to be a self-made man who needed nobody and nothing. Even when I thought I was truly happy, possessing my own company, wealth, and acclaim, I still nursed grudges and carried on feuds that existed only in my memory as I refought ancient battles with my dad.

At the time, I was devastated by my estrangement from my father and my banishment from his company. Today, I see that adversity for the wonderful gift it turned out to be: I am so thankful that instead of submitting to my father, I chose to walk away—*out from under his great shadow.* If I had joined his company on his terms, I would have continued to be his puppet. I certainly would not have become—for better or worse—the man I am today.

None of these realizations were apparent to me at the onset of my RA, however. If it hadn't been for my arthritis acting as a catalyst, I might never have become free of the emotional baggage and sour outlook on life I had inherited from my father.

The adversity of RA brought with it another cherished blessing: it forced me to reach out to my wife, Celia.

I met Celia in 1974, at her family's Florida restaurant where she worked as a waitress. I was newly divorced for the second time, wondering if I was destined never to know true love, but from our first meeting I was enchanted by Celia's beauty and charm. I asked her to marry me on our fourth date.

For someone just coming out of a bad marriage, this was wildly impulsive, of course. Yet the sense of intimacy between us was profound and immediate. There was something singular about our bond, something we could not—and still can't—fully articulate.

We set our wedding date for July 14, 1974. But I was afraid to go through with it. I made up a bunch of lame excuses, but I suppose Celia intuitively knew the real reason—that I was an emotional cripple. She agreed to push back the date to October.

I backed out of that date as well, too emotionally paralyzed to make a commitment. Celia, understandably, was furious. I thought I had lost her for good. I knew I couldn't live without her, so I managed to convince her that "the third time was the charm." On January 1, 1975, she rode to the church with me to make sure I showed up!

Although giving a guy like me all those chances might seem crazy on Celia's part, she knew exactly what she was doing. She loved me and believed in our relationship. And my wonderful wife showed the same steely determination to keep us together through the first decade of our marriage. During that time I am ashamed to say that I opened my heart only slightly to her. I didn't have a clue about how to relate to a loved one and was only comfortable unconsciously emulating my father's emotional numbness and withdrawal as I'd witnessed it growing up. I kept Celia at arm's length by being (like my father) a workaholic, subjecting our relationship to a slow, painful "death by a thousand cuts."

For ten years, in the face of my emotional frigidity, Celia was the entrepreneur in our union, creatively and at great emotional sacrifice standing by me, seeing to family matters, and gambling that we would make it.

Then came the RA. I believe that had it not been for that affliction, I would have never have opened up to Celia and to the world.

As I've explained, before RA, I considered myself to be at the center of the universe—infinitely creative, independent, invulnerable, and immortal. But it's hard to feel you're the center of the universe when your wife has to help you out of bed because your joints are rusted with arthritis, to tie your shoes for you because your fingers won't bend.

My illness forced me to realize that I not only *needed* other people, but that I was also literally at their mercy. So I began to trust Celia. My crippling illness allowed me no choice, at first . . . but then I realized just how desperately much I *wanted* to trust her.

So what's the lesson of this chapter?

Is it to simply refuse to think of yourself as being at the center of the universe? To forgive and forget past injustices inflicted upon you by others? To turn the other cheek and always look on the bright side of life?

None of the above.

I'm going to suggest something far more radical, by telling you a story about a man who suffered a terrible business reversal. Overnight, everything he had built was swept away. His financial troubles destroyed his marriage. He was back at the bottom of the heap—poor and alone, but this time, also old and tired.

You might think this tale ends in alcohol or drug

abuse, crime, or even death. However, the story has a happy ending. The man was able to rebuild his life.

I asked him how he'd managed to channel his anger and bitterness and not to drown in his adversity. He told me: "I *do* drown in my adversity—or at least I *did*—for a half hour every day.

"Each morning I'd go to the pond near me, pick up a pebble, and walk the water's circumference. During that half-hour walk I'd completely, totally, wallow in self-pity, raining down curses upon the people who'd betrayed me, swearing and crying and hating the world for the injustices I'd been dealt.

"I steeped myself in my troubles with total abandonment for my daily walk's duration, and all the while I squeezed that pebble in my hand harder and harder, as if I could squeeze all my bile into it.

"Then, as I finished my half-hour walk, approaching that point at the pond where I'd started, I tossed the pebble into the water. *That was it for the day,* I told myself. *No more anger and sadness until tomorrow.*

"Somehow, knowing I was allowing myself permission to give in totally to my troubles during my walk's duration gave me the perspective to see my way around my adversity for the rest of the day. Eventually, I no longer needed my walk. I was freed of negativity and became immersed in fresh, new personal insights and opportunities."

Try this exercise for yourself. You don't need a pond.

You don't need to walk. You don't even need a pebble (although I find that the ritual of picking one up and holding it in my hand helps me to focus and provides me permission to fully surrender myself to my negative emotions).

Give yourself a set amount of time, say, fifteen minutes to an hour, to devote yourself completely to your feelings about your troubles. Do not censor or judge yourself in any way. Tell yourself, *This is my time to be at the center of the universe; for it to be "all about me."*

When the time is up, toss away the pebble, and with it, all your self-important feelings about your adversity for that day. When dark thoughts begin to intrude, let them pass without obsessing on them, reassuring yourself that you will entertain them again at length tomorrow, during the time set aside for indulging your feelings.

If you practice this exercise, I predict that you will begin to enjoy clear-headed thinking about your adversity and forgive those you believe have wronged you . . . you'll feel your despair and hopelessness lighten . . . and you'll garner a new perspective on your many strengths. Like any self-improvement endeavor, this meditation's effectiveness is equal to the amount of effort you put into it. Try it and see what it can do.

I practiced this exercise during my battle with RA. My physical therapy was excruciating, as was my holding fast to my vow to swim fifteen miles a month. Just lowering myself into the pool was a physically exhausting ordeal. To force myself to swim I would often pretend I was out on the open sea, and it was swim or drown.

During all this, I did not (could not) keep a stiff upper lip. On the contrary, for a half hour a day I cried like a baby and wished I were dead. Sometimes I even used my half hour to daydream about my casket, the way healthier men my age might have fantasized about the details of a lusted-after sports car. I imagined *my* midlife crisis vehicle as being a tasteful, burnished mahogany casket, with polished brass trim and a red, goose down lining. (I was always feeling so cold in the water.)

Then, when the half hour was over, I cleared my mind of self-pity until the next time and got on with my life. This was my pattern for many months, until my first sign of recovery from RA.

I was sitting in the kitchen one day when I noticed that my hands did not feel as swollen. As I raised my hand in front of my face I could see light between my fingers (which had been so terribly swollen I thought my digits had been fused together).

I called out to Celia to come see. We laughed and laughed.

This brings me to the third great gift I received via the adversity of RA: the ability to comprehend the largeness of small things.

Seeing light shining between my fingers . . .

Being able to stand up by myself . . .

Experiencing a painless hour . . .

These everyday miracles brought me absolute rapture.

Can you imagine, then, what joy a sunset, a good day's work, or being able to hold Celia's hand, came to mean to me?

Life, in every sense, can become new to you as well. Your days can be filled with possibility and wonder. What it takes is your realization that your place at the center of the universe has nothing to do with your achievements, pride, or real or imagined sins, but with your ability to harness the power of adversity to learn how to react—and how not to react—to life's troubles.

Your next step to making this power your own is to understand that life's primary question, one that has been with us since antiquity, is not "Why *me?*" but "Why *not* me?"

That's the subject of the following chapter.

THREE

Don't Ask "Why *Me?*"
Instead, Ask "Why *Not* Me?"

If I were to say, "Why me?" about the bad things,
then I should have said, "Why me?" about the good
things that happened in my life.

—*Arthur Ashe*

My return to health from rheumatoid arthritis came
about not simply as a matter of physical recovery; my
spirit, too, needed to heal. At the core of these recover-
ies was a fundamental shift in the way I viewed myself.
It changed both my primary question—Why *me?*—as
well as my fundamental certitude—that I was someone
special.

In short, "Why *me?*" became "Why *not* me?"

Wrongly I had been yearning for the "good" life of

comfort, ease, happiness, money, luxury, and power, without any of the "bad" realities of sacrifice, self-discipline, and self-giving. I wanted it all for nothing. And then, when I did work hard, I became enraged that my efforts were not recognized. I had paid my dues. Where was my reward?

It never occurred to me that the adversity life handed me *was* my reward . . . that my troubles had within them the potential to raise me up to greater heights than I had ever imagined.

Many people think that the ultimate "why *me?*" story of adversity is the biblical tale of Job, but I disagree. To me, the first great adversity to crash down upon humans was the trouble that came to Adam and Eve when they were driven from the Garden of Eden. Let's review that story for a moment.

Now, I've promised you pragmatic help, not theology, so let's pare down the story of Adam and Eve to the basic plotline: naughty children are punished for disobedience by a stern father figure.

As the story goes, Adam and Eve had it made in the Garden of Eden. And if they hadn't disobeyed by eating the fruit from the tree of knowledge, we'd all still be as happy-go-lucky as trust fund babies.

But they did eat of the fruit of knowledge, and so they were banished from Eden. What had come easy to them—food, clothing, shelter—they would now have to struggle to achieve. As God says to Adam in Genesis 3,

"In the sweat of thy face shalt thou eat bread," which most would paraphrase to mean that Adam and Eve would now only have that which they could earn through the sweat of their brows. Adam and Eve (and by extension, humankind) would now experience adversity.

But let's look at God's seeming admonishment more closely. I think the bread that he speaks of is a metaphor for nourishment—and not just physical nourishment. I think God is telling Adam that from his sweat—his hard work overcoming adversity—will come nourishment in *all* its forms: physical, mental, and spiritual.

What a blessing! And not even in disguise!

Think of what Adam and Eve lost—and what they won. Sure, after they were banished from Eden, life stopped being a bowl of cherries. Instead, for them—and by extension, for us—it became a marvelous and fulfilling adventure.

Adam and Eve went from being suckled infants oblivious in the albeit comfortable but nevertheless suffocating womb of Eden to becoming the heroes of their own lives out in the wide and wonderful world. They stopped *inheriting* and began *earning.*

Now, I'll ask you, which would be more satisfying? To inherit a million dollars, or to earn it?

And I'll answer that question for you, since I've done both.

Earning is always better.

Which brings me to why the story of Adam and Eve

holds such a special place in my heart. You see, I, too, was banished from a Garden of Eden by a stern father figure . . .

Of the many vivid memories of my childhood, spending a day at my father's factory remains singular and extraordinary. I can still sense the precision and power, the perfectly controlled symmetry of efficiency that the factory embodied.

More than anything else, I recall the people who worked there, maybe a hundred or so, in the early years. Mostly immigrants—Italians, Poles, Irish—they were confident, hardworking people creating better lives for themselves.

In my eyes, these men were giants. And no one, of course, stood taller than my father. When I was at my father's factory, I remember feeling a special sense of privilege and belonging. I so wanted to be like these men when I grew up. I dreamed of one day standing among them.

But that was not to be.

To refresh your memory, as a young man in 1950, graduated from Harvard, and back from three years of military service during World War II, I was looking forward to apprenticing as a manager at my father's factory. I was shocked when he issued what I then took to be a dreadful ultimatum: either become an apprentice toolmaker on the factory floor at a far-off subsidiary, or make my own way in the world.

I chose the latter, and it was the most fortunate decision of my life. I wouldn't be who I am today if I had knuckled under to my father's demands.

Like Adam, I was banished from my Eden and all that I had ever known. Like him, I went forth to transform my life into an adventure.

Yes, I suffered some hard knocks along the way in the form of a series of dead-end jobs. Over the years, anger, bitterness, and frustration grew. Not being able to follow in my father's footsteps was incredibly demoralizing. I tried drinking away my sorrows over the fact that I believed I deserved what my father was not giving me: a stake in his company.

In short, I was the "Why *me?*" poster child, just as Adam had likely been, with the gates of Eden newly shut behind him.

Seeds of resentment grew steadily within over the perceived injustice my father had perpetrated upon me. Since I wasn't in his company, I devised a strategy to share his wealth. I met with my mother to share the details of my plan. She had great sway over my father. I knew she could convince him. And I believed I could convince her to champion my cause. She had always been doting to the point of spoiling me. With her help, streams of much needed money would soon be flowing my way.

Simply stated, my plan called for my father's company to pay dividends. Other family companies were paying dividends—why shouldn't we do the same? Those cash dividends would have made my life much easier, but they would not have been earned. And because of that, those dividends might well have been my downfall . . .

My mother was at her summer cottage in Connecticut that day I spent with her to enlist her help in convincing my father to go along with my dividends plan. That day was the biggest shock of my life. As soon as my request was out of my mouth, my sweet, adoring mother began to seethe. In essence what she said to me was, "Nobody is going to give you anything! Nobody owes you anything! Success is the gift of work, not inheritance!"

Rarely a day goes by that I don't contemplate the invaluable lesson regarding the myth of entitlement that my mother taught me that summer day in 1952. The reality of life—as opposed to the myth of the Garden of Eden—is that *you can't earn without working, and work always entails adversity*. This realization is key to understanding that the question we must ask is not "Why *me?*" but "Why *not* me?"

Today I say "Why *not* me?" to my battles with alcoholism, rheumatoid arthritis, heart disease, and any other adversity, because I know that adversity and fulfillment are two sides of the same coin called life. You simply can't have one without the other.

I say "Why *not* me?" because everything I've struggled so hard to earn is far sweeter to me than if it had been given to me as an inheritance. I am so grateful to have been tested by life, and not to have been King Midas. Everything he touched turned to gold, but that seeming blessing turned out to be a curse when food and drink were transformed before he could partake of them. Even his beloved child was transformed into a cold, lifeless statue by his affectionate touch.

When we rid ourselves of the debilitating anger that comes from our sense of being *singled* out by adversity, the question that we must ask ourselves can only sensibly be "Why *not* me?"

In life, virtually everyone is confronted by troubles of one kind or another. It is not what *happens* to you, but how you *respond* that's meaningful. As Harold Kushner writes in his powerful and moving book, *When Bad Things Happen to Good People:*

> I don't believe that an earthquake that kills thousands of innocent victims without reason is an act of God. It is an act of nature. Nature is morally blind, without values. It churns along, following its own ways, not caring who or what gets in the way . . . For me, the earthquake is not an "act of God." The act of God is the courage of people to rebuild their lives after the earthquake, and the rush of others to help them in whatever way they can.[1]

There are over six billion people on the face of the Earth. Virtually every one of them is currently enduring some form of adversity, from professional setbacks, relationship problems, and varying degrees of physical or mental illness, to misplaced car keys.

Can you imagine the din to heaven if everyone experiencing some degree of difficulty in life cried out, "Why *me?*"

And conversely, the worldwide serenity if each of us merely shrugged and smiled, "Why *not* me?"

Coming around to thinking "Why *not* me?" is part and parcel of acknowledging that you truly aren't at the center of the universe—that pernicious notion that you are Hercules with the world on your shoulders—and entitled to all the privileges and responsibilities that come with that status. Changing your perspective and perception to "Why *not* me?" can provide you with a tremendous sense of inner peace and personal satisfaction.

So how do you make the transition?

The answer is surprising. It's to be *self*-ish—which I define as being concerned with one's *inner self,* as opposed to regular, old *selfish,* which I consider as being stingy and mean in a Scrooge-like sense. And so . . .

THE TRULY *SELF*-ISH PERSON PUTS HIMSELF *FIRST,* BY PUTTING HIMSELF *LAST.*

The next time you're running late driving to an appointment, instead of hurrying, purposely *slow down.* Let somebody merge into the traffic ahead of you.

By giving up three seconds of your life, you'll change your entire perspective on your own situation. You'll no longer be obsessed with being late or feeling like a victim of circumstances. Instead of wondering "Why *me?*" you'll bask in the warm glow that comes from doing someone else a favor.

So let somebody merge . . .

Let someone ahead of you if you have a shopping cart full of groceries and she or he only has a couple of items . . .

Or just hold the door for somebody . . .

By giving yourself the pleasure of fighting the primitive "me first" response that many of us experience in these types of situations, you ultimately *are* putting yourself *first* (in terms of experiencing less stress and anger) by putting yourself *last.* Even more important, you're changing the way you think from that of being a victim (Why *me?*) to being the master of your adversity (Why *not* me?).

When you get to wherever you were going a few seconds later, nobody will care, but that small gift of compassion and generosity you gave to that other person will come back to you many-fold in terms of peaceful perspective on your problems. Try it and see.

The question next arises: How do you keep yourself from succumbing to a mob mentality when you find yourself in a murky sea of thoughtlessness and rudeness? *How do you give when everybody is a taker?*

It's a difficult challenge, no doubt about it.

In such a case, you have to be *extra self*-ish.

The trick I use is to put myself on a mental balcony and look down upon the maddening throngs. This perspective reminds me that I will not benefit or in any way feel better by lashing out, and that I will not be like those losers who are giving away that which is most precious—their inner serenity—for the cheap and fleeting high that comes from rage.

I think of it as a lot like being addicted to smoking. (Yes, I was addicted to cigarettes, as well as to booze.) You succumb to road rage, for instance *(I'll show that sonofabitch he can't cut me off)*, just like you succumb to smoking a cigarette. But that cigarette satiates you only for a little while and then you crave another. And then another.

It's exactly the same thing when you succumb to the "Why *me?*" entitlement notion that you are at the center of the universe. It leads you to lash out at others through road rage to strangers, thoughtless and cruel remarks to friends and loved ones, and all the other tiny and large acts of cruelty we perpetrate on others and ourselves.

You keep needing that rage-fueled high, which never

lasts and usually brings with it the terrible downer of knowing *you* were really the one who just behaved like a sonofabitch (often in front of your disapproving spouse or bewildered and frightened children), and so you vow never to do it again.

Many of us have vowed, "This is my last cigarette," and come to mean it.

Some of us have had to say, "No more drinking," and carry through on our promise.

All of us, sooner or later, need to take the oath, *No more blaming the world for my troubles . . .* It takes real willpower to quit this, or any, bad habit (boy, does it ever!), but it can be done.

The question is, *Will we do it?*

Given my personal history with alcoholism, the topic of willpower and self-discipline holds a special fascination for me. Through my involvements with the Weatherhead East Asian Institute at Columbia University and the Weatherhead Center for International Affairs at Harvard—creations of our family foundation, which I will tell you about later—I have discovered that what Eastern philosophies have to teach us is germane to our subject of mastering the power of adversity in daily life.

Consider what the Vietnamese martial artist Tri Thong Dang tells us in his book *Beyond the Known: The Ultimate Goal of the Martial Arts:* "Abstaining from matters from which others cannot abstain and performing deeds that others cannot perform are the business of the martial-arts practitioner."[2]

Think about that. There's nothing in that quote that's implicitly about fighting with adversaries. But there's a ton in there about disciplining yourself to triumph in all your inner battles against adversity. We're so used to what we see in kung-fu movies that we think martial arts is all about beating up a gang of thugs.

But what if the "ultimate goal of the martial arts" is not to develop the ability to break boards with the edge of your hand, but to become the type of person who is disciplined enough to be polite in traffic?

Jesus said it succinctly in his Sermon on the Mount: "By their fruits ye shall know them." I believe Jesus meant that if you want to identify those individuals who understood his teachings, and mastering adversity is certainly a part of that, you can do so by observing how they behave in the interactions (and irritations) of daily life.

Remember, all problems in your life—large and small—can and should be approached and resolved in the same manner. (You walk across the street and you walk across America the same way—the latter just takes longer than the former.)

So if you really want to master the power of adversity, make this your test: gauge your burgeoning mastery by your ability to keep your cool or your inclination to lose it in the smallest vexing situations—

like at the grocery's express checkout register, when the person in front of you has a full shopping cart.

At my factory, when we're engaged in engineering a new product, we start small, perfecting the manufacturing procedure, and then increase our production volume to commercial levels. In business, this time-tested process is known as "scaling-up."

Start mastering your adversity by dealing positively with the smallest problems you encounter and then "scale up" that response to effectively deal with the mega-adversity in your life.

Of course, adversity has a ton of tricks up its sleeve to beat you. Its greatest stratagem to avoiding being tamed is to distract us with our own heartfelt, masochistic desire to view ourselves as victims.

For example—and this relates back to the notion of being at the center of the universe—many of us have been caught in a traffic jam. Eventually, when we inch by the horrendous accident that was the cause of the backup, we *still* manage to remain so egocentric as to curse the situation in terms of our own minor misfortune as to be late.

It's a terrific con on adversity's part, because if our troubles can get us thinking "Why *me?*" we'll be too immersed in self-pity to whip adversity into line and make it work for us.

My wife, Celia, calls it having a "pity party." She's all

for it, as long as you have your party and get over it. But when I was stricken with the paralyzing pain of rheumatoid arthritis my bed-ridden pity party *lasted over a year*—until one morning while I was lying in bed I turned over and found Celia standing over me.

"Al," she began. I may have lifted my head and groaned.

"Al," she repeated, more firmly. "You've got to get out of bed!"

Perhaps I groaned again, this time with sufficient guttural resonance to remind her of my unrelenting pain.

"Al, if you want to save yourself and if you want to save our marriage, you *have* to get out of bed."

Anger was my first reaction: *didn't she care about the depths of my pain?*

My second reaction, even if it was not fully understood at the time, was: *she truly loves me.*

It was my third reaction that was the most curious. Her words slipped formation in my mind, until: "I *have* to do it" (getting out of bed) became "I have *it* to do."

You see, mastering the power of adversity, first and last, is all about choice. First you *choose* to do it . . . and you continue to *do* it by carrying on with your series of choices.

If you're muttering to yourself, "That's just semantics . . . foolish word play . . .," think again. Your adversity is real. It cannot change. But it can be *transformed.*

The Zen master Thich Nhat Hanh makes this point while talking about anger (and adversity and anger are invariably intertwined), in his guide to meditation, *Peace Is Every Step: The Path of Mindfulness in Everyday Life:*

> When anger is born in us, we can be aware that anger is an energy in us, and we can accept that energy in order to transform it into another kind of energy. When we have a compost bin filled with organic material which is decomposing and smelly, we know that we can transform the waste into beautiful flowers . . . We know that anger can be a kind of compost, and that it is within its power to give birth to something beautiful. We need anger the way the organic gardener needs compost. If we know how to accept our anger, we already have some peace and joy. Gradually we can transform anger completely into peace, love, and understanding.[3]

Why view a problem as a problem? Think creatively and banish negativity! What I say to myself when faced with a problem in order to transmute dark energy into the light of creativity (well, sometimes I mutter it, but I say it, just the same), is:

"Hain't we having fun."

Not "Hain't we got problems," but "Hain't we having fun."

Do you think that's simplistic?

Well, so is turning on the light when you enter a dark room, but doesn't that light make all the difference in the world to keep you from stumbling?

In the comic strip *L'il Abner,* Joe Btfsplk was a sad sack who went everywhere with a dark cloud over his head. Why not step out of that angry cloud into the serene sunlight?

It's absolutely your choice to do so . . . All it takes is a change of mindset to see how your journey of resolving your adversity can be as enriching and illuminating as ultimately solving the problem. That's when you *know* you're mastering the power of adversity.

To further illuminate this point, I'll offer you another quote from the East, this time, from a poetic volume called *Hagakure: The Book of the Samurai,* written in the 1700s by a warrior named Yamamoto Tsunetomo:

> There is something to be learned from a rainstorm. When meeting with a sudden shower, you try not to get wet and run quickly along the road. But doing such things as passing under the eaves of houses, you still get wet. When you are resolved from the beginning, you will not be perplexed, though you still get the same soaking. This understanding extends to everything.[4]

Isn't that a profound quote about recognizing your adversity when it comes along—which it will, as inevitably and frequently as the rain falls upon the earth—but not being "perplexed" by it?

In other words, dealing with it in a forthright and positive manner . . .

To recap my advice to you from this chapter:

Don't ask "Why *me?*" Ask "Why *not* me?"—The battles of adversity and rewards of fulfillment are two sides of the same coin called life. You simply can't have one without the other.

It is luckier to *earn* than to *receive*—The rewards of work are far sweeter than those bestowed on us by fortune . . . and work always entails adversity.

Be *self*-ish and put yourself *first*, by putting yourself *last*—Build your discipline and gain a powerful new perspective on life by denying the primitive "me first" impulse.

Never think "I *have* to do it." Instead think "I have *it* to do."—Mastering adversity is all about choice. First you *choose* to do it . . . and you continue to *do* it by continuing your series of choices.

Measure your mastery of adversity by your capacity to show generosity and compassion in vexing circumstances small and large—Test your "business model" for dealing with little adversities in your life, and then "scale up" your effective responses to handle major problems.

Transform *"Hain't we got problems"* into *"Hain't*

we having fun."—Change your mindset concerning adversity. Think creatively and banish negativity!

If you view your life and move through the world in this way, you will come to see that there are no problems—merely challenges and puzzles that are sometimes entertaining and sometimes tedious, but always enthralling and filled with opportunities from which you can profit materially, physically, mentally, and spiritually.

FOUR

I Suffer Passes . . .
I Suffered Never Passes

There is something beautiful about all scars of whatever nature. A scar means the hurt is over, the wound is closed and healed, done with.

—Harry Crews

Dr. Leslie Weatherhead,[5] my distant cousin and one of Britain's leading Methodist ministers, beautifully stated the theme of this chapter in his book, *The Significance of Silence:*

In earlier years I believed that God intended man to be happy in the ordinary sense of the word: free from pain . . . I now feel . . . that God willed the circumstances in which suffering is pretty certain for most of us. Only a few lucky

ones escape . . . And are they really lucky? . . . I
am probably not speaking to anybody over thirty-
five who has not experienced something in the
way of physical or mental suffering, and I think if
I could ask you . . . now that the suffering has
passed, whether you wish it had been avoided,
you would say that you are glad that you passed
through it.[6]

What do you do to exercise? Do you run?

Back before my rheumatoid arthritis, when I was
regularly doing 10K runs, I always found the first few
minutes before I warmed up to be complete physical
torture: a veritable symphony of aches and pains.

Now I swim. Every day, sometimes kicking and
screaming, I have the pool to be in. The water's so cold
when I first get in that the prospect of swimming fifty
to one hundred laps is incredibly daunting.

However, whether it's running, swimming, weight
training, or any other form of exercise, once you get
past those first ten minutes or so and warm up, the
endorphins begin to surge. It's the "runner's high"
release of chemicals in the brain that brings such bliss,
but that can only be earned by enduring the physical
exertion.

Tackling adversity is like tackling exercise. Once you
get over the "warm-up" period and the endorphins
begin to surge, you'll take pleasure in tackling your
problem.

Why? Because it is so much more pleasurable to be the hammer than the nail! When you tackle a problem you're taking control, you're the hammer. When you let adversity fester, you're the nail . . . the victim.

What's more, just as my completing the first few laps in the pool provides me with the confidence to know I can meet that challenge the next time, each instance of adversity that I tackle strengthens my self-confidence so that I can solve any problem that I might encounter.

This spiritual strength builds up day by day, just like your physical strength through your exercise routine. I like to think of it as a tempering process: just as a blade remains tempered long after the fire that scorched it has faded away, we grow stronger through the tempering effects of adversity in our lives. Nietzsche nailed it on the head when he remarked: whatever doesn't kill you makes you stronger.

This tempering effect does not come free, of course. Just as with physical exercise, dealing with adversity involves the absolute necessity of moving *through* and finally *beyond* the initial pain in order to achieve your goal. With exercise, that goal is health benefits. With tackling adversity, the goal is to realize the benefits of a rich and rewarding life.

We can further use the analogy between exercise and adversity for our edification. For instance, every time I give in to an excuse to skip a workout, I avoid that day's initial aches and pains, but I grow physically weaker as a result. Accordingly, every time I refuse to deal with a problem, I momentarily avoid the immediacy of unpleasantness—but I can never forestall the inevitable consequences of letting adversity linger.

Take swimming. The longer I procrastinate, the harder it becomes to eventually get into the pool—and I know I have it to do, sooner or later. In the same way, the longer I postpone dealing with an adversity, the harder it will be to eventually confront it. Even worse, by avoiding adversities, thus allowing them to accumulate, I find myself dragging behind me a long bag of trash filled with resentment, guilt, anger, disappointment, and hurt.

Now let's be positive. Exercise builds physical strength and flexibility. The payoff to dealing with adversity with diligence and honesty is that it similarly builds and limbers up the mind and spirit, enabling us to experience the greater possibilities of life.

My long, painful, and often uncertain battle with rheumatoid arthritis, for instance, taught me not so much what was wrong with my life, but what was generally right about it. My previous view of success— mostly inherited from my father or borrowed from other luminaries—was myopic in its materialism and lust for power.

Celia, through her love, prodded me to my emotional epiphany, but it was the adversity of RA, in effect, that forced my hand. Which existence was it going to be for me? Living alone, hidden in fear, locked away in a jail of my own making? Or living with boundless love? By choosing the latter, a bright horizon spread before me. My physical health problems become more tolerable as my mind became centered.

The holistic relationship between mind, body, and spirit was first recognized in the East, but today is well understood by Western science. The ancient Japanese samurai code of conduct held in high esteem virtues like modesty, gratitude, courtesy, self-control, compassion, perseverance, and indomitable spirit.

In the West we tend to think of these virtues as the "icing on the cake"—the grease that keeps society running more or less smoothly. It's something we do, or are supposed to do, for the benefit of the other person . . .

What, for example, the samurai code of conduct understood is that the practice of these virtues is primarily a *self*-ish act (using my definition of putting yourself *first* by putting yourself *last*) that can benefit one's mind, body, and spirit. How you choose to conduct yourself influences how you feel physically and how you perceive the world mentally and spiritually. The samurais practiced these virtues for their own benefit. They couldn't have cared less about the other person . . .

What the samurais and Zen masters also understood—and many of us do not—is that adhering to these virtues is essential if we wish to take advantage of the tempering process that adversity affords us to evolve in life.

Allow me to share with you my understanding of each of these potentially holistic virtues—I call them the seven *self*-ish virtues—as they pertain to the martial art I wish to teach you: the art of mastering the power of adversity.

Modesty: Before rheumatoid arthritis I considered myself master of my own universe—tested, infinitely creative, independent, invulnerable, and immortal. Of course, in those days I was quite the opposite—a man with a heart that was icy-cold and barricaded behind walls of pride. Thus, the adversity of rheumatoid arthritis was a blessing because it forced me, for the first time in my life, to humbly acknowledge my need for others. In a very real sense, my illness put me at others' mercy. Due to Celia's unwavering love, my trust in her over time blossomed into a deep sharing of our lives, where before there had only been my dominance.

> *Find the modesty within you that in times of adversity will allow you to reach out to others for help. These relationships will nourish and sustain you long after your adversity has been conquered—that same adversity that led you to open your heart in the first place.*

Gratitude: The adversity of my illnesses (alcoholism, RA, and heart disease), taught me to be grateful for the joyous largesse of the small things in life. Throughout my bout of RA, for instance, despite medication, the waves of pain were often overwhelming. As I began to heal, just being able to stand on my feet for a few moments filled me with gratitude for my tiny victory. As time passed and I grew ever stronger, I continued to take grateful joy in that which I had always taken for granted: being able to travel—either across the ocean or simply out for a stroll after dinner on a summer evening.

Life can be new for you and pregnant with possibility and wonder, when you accept adversity's great gift: your ability to appreciate and be grateful for all the good things in your life, both large and small.

Courtesy and Self-Control: I lump these two together when it comes to the subject of mastering adversity. Both these virtues relate back to the act of putting yourself first by putting yourself last through acts of small courtesies like allowing somebody to merge ahead of you in traffic.

The reservoir of spiritual strength you build up day by day exercising courtesy and self-control when dealing with trivial annoyances and problems will come into play when large-scale adversity looms and life becomes really difficult.

Compassion: You already know that a great adversity in my life has been my anguished relationship with my father. This adversity has caused me pain beyond belief, and may have even been responsible for the other adversities in my life, such as my physical illnesses. But without that estrangement, I might never have developed the capacity for compassion, which, more than any other quality makes me who I am today.

In December 1966, my father made it known that he was suffering from cancer. He summoned me to his large office, lined with awards, memorabilia, and all the trappings and totems of his long and illustrious career. As I entered, he was sitting behind his massive oak desk. So many times through the years I had seen my father behind this very desk, but as a proud, strong, vibrant giant. Now, here he was, hunched over, wasting away. He rose slowly and painfully from his creased leather chair and said, "Al, I'm dying. I want you to take care of our family and company for me when I'm gone."

Then he did something he had never done before: he held out his hand. I am so grateful that through adversity I had developed enough to be able to set aside my grievances and accept that proffered handshake. At long last, my father and I were reconciled . . . For me, it was the greatest gift of all . . .

The sharp blade of adversity severs us from the facade of false images we create for ourselves. As one by one they are whittled away, we become more vulnerable and more compassionate. Next, by setting us

*on the hard, steep path toward self-improvement,
adversity tempers us for the day when we will have the
opportunity to demonstrate our compassion by choosing to be strong on behalf of those who are weak. Our
ultimate reward is the opening of our hearts to love.*

Perseverance: In business and relationships, adversity is a constant. Take positive action with the ideas
you believe are the wisest actions at the moment, knowing full well that things may change for the better or
worse tomorrow. Remember that the Declaration of
Independence tells us that "all men are created equal,
that they are endowed by their Creator with certain
unalienable rights, that among these are life, liberty, and
the pursuit of happiness." I think the Founding Fathers
were sticklers on their choice of words. Please note that
they did not write that we have the right to *life, liberty,
and happiness.* They stuck in the pesky word *pursuit.* To
me, "to pursue" means "to chase." So we've got the right
to chase happiness. Personally, I don't think we're ever
supposed to catch it. Because if we did, what would we
do next? And as soon as we started worrying about *that,*
would we still be happy?

*Accept adversity as your constant shadow, but
keep your shadow behind you, not in front of you, by
persevering and moving forward.*

Indomitable Spirit: When you think about it, your pursuit of happiness is like being on a treadmill. As with most exercise devices, this treadmill has some easy levels to get you started, but the levels inevitably become more difficult. In life, you may work hard in pursuit of a goal (say, a new car), and you get it, but the car is just a symbol for whatever it is that you really want, and so it's back on the treadmill in pursuit of the next goal, and then the next. The adversity seems to never stop. That's as it's supposed to be, because enjoyment and happiness are not synonymous. I can enjoy life and still be unhappy. For example, I can enjoy tackling a problem, but the very fact that I'm motivated to do so means that I am not happy with the status quo (if I were, I'd just leave the problem unresolved).

If perseverance equips you to continually confront your adversity and so ever improve, indomitable spirit makes you not mind—and even enjoy—the endless pursuit of an ultimately unreachable ideal.

Physical exercise tempers the body through repetition. One of the pleasures of any workout routine or game is finally mastering the basics and letting the training take over so you can focus on the subtleties.

After three-quarters of a century of swimming, I no longer need to think about the mechanics of it. I move through the water automatically, executing with whatever grace and ease I can muster a highly complex routine, learned and improved upon throughout the years, and retained, for instant use, in my subconscious. It's called "muscle memory," a skill never forgotten and always on call.

Make the tips and techniques in this chapter part of your "muscle memory"—your second nature—to leverage to the greatest degree the tempering process offered by adversity. Instill into your life the virtues we've discussed and adversity will temper you for the better.

As the French proverb says, *"To suffer passes away, but to have suffered never passes."* The gain of the experience is ours forever—but only if we bring ourselves to accept and acknowledge it.

Start by cultivating the seven *self*-ish virtues and use them to confront and conquer your bitterness and anger when adversity rears its ugly head to taunt and cut you.

All of us have endured the same wounds in life, merely delivered in differing circumstances by different means. I'm not offering you a band aid. I'm providing you a way to close your wounds.

Don't go through life patched up due to whatever troubles you've experienced.

Go through life healed and strengthened—by adversity.

FIVE

Adversity Builds Walls
for You to Tear Down

I have heard there are troubles of more than one kind.
Some come from ahead and some come from behind.
But I've bought a big bat. I'm all ready you see.
Now my troubles are going to have troubles with me!

—*Dr. Seuss*

When you let adversity build walls around you, you have the safety of those walls.

But you can't see out.

And nobody can see in.

My illnesses gave me the wakeup calls I needed in this regard. Until stricken with rheumatoid arthritis I thought I could conquer anything and everything.

But getting sick the way I did—first with RA and

then with heart disease—showed me that I needed help if I was going to make it, and I became willing to ask for it. This was something I had to learn how to do, and I'm glad I did, because it changed my life.

However, I might not have been ready to ask for help in overcoming heart disease if the adversity of RA hadn't introduced me to the concept. I won't go so far as to say that things happen for a reason. Maybe they do and maybe they don't, and anyway, that kind of question is beyond the scope of this book. I do believe that when things happen—seemingly bad things, especially—we can choose to profit from our experience of them.

For instance, I was able to leverage my terrible experience of RA to help me conquer my heart disease. In the parlance of business . . . I took the sweat equity I had built up by mastering adversity through my experience with RA and used it as my down payment to help me recover from heart disease.

Think about your experiences with adversity in this manner. Create a spiritual profit-and-loss sheet as relates to each adversity you have experienced or are currently experiencing in life:

- What has your adversity *cost* you?
- What has it *earned* you?
- How have you *profited* by it?

It's my guess that with the right perspective—the

perspective I hope my book is providing—you will come to realize that the sum of your experiences added up in your adversity ledger puts you in the *black,* not the *red.*

In my case, confronting my heart attack was simply another milestone in my journey through a high-walled maze, with my ultimate destination being the mastery of my adversity. I wish I could brag to you that I realized all this at the time, but the walls of adversity can form a confusing labyrinth. When you're lost in a maze you may think you're heading in the correct direction, when really you are merely going around in circles until you arrive at yet another dead end.

My heart attack in 1989 came when—or because—I had learned some wrong lessons from my battle with rheumatoid arthritis. That summer, feeling nearly recovered from RA, I was rowing nearly forty miles a week in my effort to get my body into shape. Thinking I was in top-flight physical condition after that summer of rowing, I then began an intense swimming regimen—never mind that I had taken a six-month layoff from swimming. After several 2,500-yard swims, I began experiencing shoulder pains that got worse and worse, radiating down through my arms. Meanwhile, I was eating like a horse, except that horses don't indulge in a steady diet of the richest, most fat-laden foods imaginable.

I thought exercise—which had saved me from RA—

could and would protect me from everything, but I was wrong. Dead wrong, nearly!

There's no need to bore you with the medical details of my heart attack. Suffice to say that like any heart attack, it was no day at the beach.

What's important about it as relates to the matter before us, is that when this latest major adversity felled me I initially panicked, and then I despaired. To find myself laid up in bed again—*again!*—so soon after having put behind me those bedridden years crippled by RA, broke my spiritual heart even as my physical heart was in need of repair.

Talk about wandering in a high-walled maze! I truly did feel like I had spent all that hard effort believing I was traveling to my intended destination, only to find that I had walked in a circle and ended up back where I'd started.

That's when my sweat equity derived from my experience with RA came through for me. It provided me the strength to chip away at the walls of my latest labyrinth, so that I could begin to catch glimmers of where I needed to go.

This time, right away I sought help.

First, of course, from Celia. Unlike my struggle with RA—and certainly as a result of it—I did not push her away. I sought safety in her arms, and as my heart opened up to my wife I think it truly began to heal on every level.

And as the shock abated, I reached out for more help.

In 1990 I read the book *Dr. Dean Ornish's Program for Reversing Heart Disease,* and wrote to him, offering to fly to San Francisco and enlist in his pioneer study. That highly select group had long been doing the heart disease reversal program and could not accept new participants, but shortly after our exchange, Dr. Ornish offered his first heart reversal retreat in California. I applied and was accepted.

Ornish's theory was simple. With a combination of lifestyle changes, including a healthy diet, stress reduction, and exercise, the progression of heart disease could be halted and perhaps reversed. More than anything, Ornish opened the world's eyes to the notion that heart disease was not just a physical problem but a holistic one.

According to him, it is equally as possible to shut down the heart by denying intimacy as it is by consuming fatty foods. Surgery and drugs are often essential when one is experiencing the heart attack, but they do nothing to resolve the underlying cause. A coronary bypass is just that: a *bypass* of the problem.

Ornish taught that reversing heart disease demands enormous patience, love, and understanding . . . a union of mind, body, and spirit . . .

Those words resonated within me as the sweat equity earned through my previous adversity kicked in, and the walls began to come down. I at last began to draw the right conclusions about adversity—how I had been responding to it and how my responses were changing:

- My ostracism from my father's company had ultimately caused me to abandon my false images of who I was and what I deserved, versus what I had to earn.

- Alcoholism and rheumatoid arthritis had humbled me by rubbing my nose in my terrible isolation, stripping me down until my only choice was to reach out to others.

- Now heart disease was presenting me with yet another opportunity to understand myself and the world around me in a more loving fashion.

What made this particular illness/adversity unique and especially intimidating was that it carried with it the risk of death. While all the other adversities in my life had been serious, none before this one was potentially fatal.

So my heart attack—more than any other problem I'd faced—was a cold shower that woke me to the staggering realization: the adversity we perceive as an exterior problem—like a heart attack—is often really the symptom of a problem deep within ourselves. It is only by tearing down the walls of adversity that those deep-rooted issues will at long last be revealed.

In my case, I learned that my heart condition was not a matter of the "heart attacked" as much as my heart attacking *me* in retribution for the festering knots and thorns in my life.

Tearing down the walls of adversity and reaching out to others isn't and shouldn't be the only way to progress. You can also lure yourself out of adversity's shadow by finding something—anything—you think you can do to tackle the problem you're confronting.

We'll talk more about choices in the following chapter. For now, let me emphasize that *any* step you take will begin to transform your *wall* into a *bridge* to help you escape your labyrinth and reach spectacular vistas of self-potential.

Your first step is to convince yourself that you have thought through your avenue of action and that it is the right thing for you to do at this moment. Not necessarily an hour, day, week, month, or year from now—but *right now.*

Take my drinking. It didn't matter that I could go weeks, months, even a year or more without going on a binge, because sooner or later (usually when I thought nobody would be the wiser), I'd disappear into some hotel room and hit the bottle nonstop.

In 1966, I started going to Alcoholics Anonymous

meetings. Then I prided myself on being only a periodic drunk. I was, I thought, better than "that drunken slob lying in the gutter."

The beginnings of my sobriety and my life in AA commenced when I spent seven days in Rosary Hall, a retreat for recovering alcoholics at Saint Vincent Charity Hospital in Cleveland. There I went through basic training for alcoholics. Since then, I have been sober, and to those of us in AA that means one day at a time or shorter periods of time if necessary.

Several years later at an AA meeting where I gave my lead, Jack Ball, a thirty-year member of the organization commented, "Al, you're nothing more than a goddamned drunk who's periodically sober."

There it was. The bald-faced truth. And that meant no more lying to myself! No more running and no more hiding from myself.

What's the right first or next step for you to take to free yourself from the prison of your adversity? Not tomorrow or next week or next year, but right now? Simply take the time to marshal your arguments about your choice of strategy and detail them to yourself the way you would to persuade another person. Your way will come clear to you. In addition, you'll be amazed at the peace of mind you will experience . . . a peace that comes from knowing you're doing the right thing to the best of your ability.

The walls of your adversity might seem too high to

scale. Never mind. Don't look up and don't look down. Look straight ahead, find that first foothold, and climb. Soon that wall will become merely a stepping stone to the next phase of your life—and *(surprise!)* your next adversity. At that point, recall the concept of sweat equity and realize that when you leverage your learning from adversity past and present there is *no failure and no wasted time.*

This is a lesson I try to teach at my factory as I mentor the new generation of management that has taken over the day-to-day leadership of my business. I stress that the important thing is to have fun moving forward, addressing the inevitable mistakes as they arise, but not obsessing about dead ends or what might go wrong in the future.

It all comes back to Rule 12 in the list in chapter 1 that I devised to help you put adversity to work:

ADVERSITY ALWAYS GRANTS A CHANCE TO CREATIVELY RESOLVE THE PROBLEM.

In my experience, the first creative solution or decision that comes to me is usually the right one . . . It's that idea, plain and simple, that feels correct in my gut.

Once you've been *creative* and come up with your solution, it's time to be *innovative.*

Throw your ideas against the wall and see what

sticks, remembering that there's no such thing as a mistake if you learn something from your actions.

As I've already said, worrying too much about the future can trap you in mental quicksand. The more you flail, the deeper you sink.

How do you get out? The same way you escape from *real* quicksand. Relax, so that you float to the surface. Then, one move at a time, propel yourself to safety. Of course, it also doesn't hurt to apply one of the most important lessons from this book: reach out to others to help you escape from your quagmire of adversity. Chances are, the next time around, *you'll* be the one doing the helping.

You truly can bring down your personal walls built with the bricks of adversity and venture forth into a bright new dawn of self-potential. I've shown you the keys to your prison.

Now it's up to you to use them.

SIX

Running Away Never Helps

> You can't run away from trouble. There ain't no
> place that far.
>
> —*Uncle Remus*

Alcoholics Anonymous taught me that the easiest
and most useless response for an alcoholic is a geographical cure: *hide!* Go somewhere else. Temporarily
the problems seem to diminish, but wherever you go,
your problems always go with you. Such an escape is a
delusion. Follow its path and eventually you will
plunge over a cliff—even if that cliff happens to over-
look the beautiful, blue Pacific Ocean.

In 1967, following my father's death from cancer, I
expended most of my energy trying to save his company from the subpar management of the executive

team that had taken over. It was tiring, lonesome, and thankless work.

My pledge to my father and sufficient company stock forced the new management at the Weatherhead Company to tolerate me, but they did not do so warmly. They also knew nothing about running a manufacturing company—they were accountants, first and last—but they had the controlling shares to veto any course of action I might recommend.

During all of 1967 and the early months of 1968, I negotiated a merger of the Weatherhead Company with a larger company with similar product lines. The deal was for the larger company to acquire Weatherhead for cash and stock.

Weatherhead directors shot down my deal, with tragic results for the company and its stockholders. At the initial public offering in 1968, Weatherhead common stock sold for $24.50 per share and was trading in the low to mid-$30s per share. In a short span of time the stock market hammered Weatherhead common. Stockholders took a bloodbath, losing 90 percent of their money because of flagrant mismanagement!

On the front page of *The Cleveland Press* from November 25, 1970, the headline "Weatherhead to Shut Down" confirmed the company's imminent death.

It was during this dismal period in my life that the vision of my late mother appeared to me. I was jogging along the embankment of Horseshoe Lake, an idyllic, tree-lined pond in Cleveland. The crisp, pine-scented air propelled me forward, the rhythm of my gait serving to temporarily drown out my disappointment in life. With the wind rustling my jacket I jogged to escape my personal and professional humiliations.

Mother had died a decade before, but I still thought of her every day. And then there she was, standing before me on the jogging trail. I stopped short, gasping, thinking initially that this was all just an hallucination brought on by my drinking, but I'd been on the wagon at this point for a long while . . .

"My darling son," she said, "You are being honest and fair. I have faith in you."

And she was gone.

I've never had the vision again, but the love it engendered in me lasts to this day.

At the time, however, I was able to take little solace from the notion that my mother might have been forgiving me for failing to fulfill the promise I had made to my father regarding saving his company. I couldn't forgive *myself* for breaking that promise. To me, my default was just another example of my failings in life.

After my scuttled merger deal there was nothing more I could do. I'd had the wisdom during the initial public offering to sell some of my stock. When I did, management was quick to suggest I take the money and run, striking at me where I was most vulnerable: my tattered, corrosive self-image as a drunk and as a maverick who had early on nearly deserted my father.

At this point I had already started my AA life with six other drunks at Rosary Hall, the rehabilitation center for alcoholics at Cleveland's Saint Vincent Charity Hospital. I lived my AA life, one day at a time. But my self-esteem at that point was so low that my enemies on the Weatherhead board were able to persuade me that they were right.

After all, once a drunk, always a drunk . . .

And so I left Cleveland, feeling emotionally and physically exhausted. In comparison to the chaos, dissonance, and resentment I was enduring, California had a beckoning call. I was still smarting from my failure to keep my promise to my father. I had done my best, but the resistance to new ideas by those who held the real power at Weatherhead had beaten me down. California represented peace and a new start. *But there is a difference between moving toward a new goal and moving to escape an old reality.*

This was arguably the lowest point in my life, to date.

Celia was still in my future. I was now an AA newcomer and just barely hanging on. And pressing down upon me was the burden of my having reconciled with my father at long last, only to come to believe that I had ultimately let him down by failing to save his company.

What kind of man was I? And wouldn't a nice, iced martini take the edge off the pain?

As you can imagine, my despairing thoughts almost killed me. I was nearly swept away by my barely suppressed addiction to booze, my loneliness, and the fiercely competing compulsions within me to accomplish great things and to escape.

In short, I was a wreck. However, it was all this terrible adversity that ultimately saved me.

The turning point came on the Southern California coast as I stood on a green knoll in the backyard of a lovely residential property overlooking the sweeping panorama of the sparkling blue Pacific Ocean. In my pocket was the down payment for this wonderful home. For me, California and this house were going to make everything all better. But as the saying goes: *wherever you go, there you are . . .*

As I looked across the manicured lawn to the waves breaking on the rocks and felt the salt air on my face, I knew I was only kidding myself that things had really changed. This so-called new start was nothing more than a self-imposed witness protection program.

I realized I had to go back to face my demons and beat them once and for all. In this way, I was lucky to see adversity for what it was, despite its attempt to duck its ugly countenance beneath those roiling Pacific whitecaps.

It was not my ingenuity, character, or brilliance that

made the difference. If anything, it was a matter of timing. I was ready for the epiphany, and so it came:

WHEN IT COMES TO ADVERSITY, THERE'S NO SUCH THING AS GREENER PASTURES.

Geographical cures only change the external circumstances of adversity. The interior roads of negative motivation and emotion remain unexplored. Real change—a transformation that can be the blessing of adversity—isn't brought about by changing our *surroundings*. It is the product of changing *ourselves*.

People facing a hard set of circumstances often make one of two fatal mistakes:

- They either believe their present adversity is so severe that there is no hope of repair, rendering the future worthless;

- Or they believe that some sort of *future* repair can neutralize their *present* turmoil.

The first choice is one of self-pity; the second is one of denial.

Neither approach works. My own adversities have taught me that when dealing with problems we must be . . .

Creative—We need to use all of our powers of imagination to see beyond our overwhelming feelings of despair, disappointment, rejection, and loneliness.

Patient—Our urge to resolve the adversity as quickly as possible impels us to rush away from the pain. This is why I went to California. It's the *fight or flight* syndrome, and flight always seems easier and quicker. I didn't want to do the arduous and painful work of mastering my adversity. I just wanted *out.*

Impatience also seduces us into thinking that only one solution to our problems exists. But for every problem there is always more than one solution. These myriad solutions unfold like the petals of a flower when you take the time to explore your adversity slowly and thoroughly.

In California, for instance, I realized that trying a geographic cure for my problems was far worse than useless; it was actually dangerous. The more escapism is sought in such circumstance, the greater becomes the pain. In this way your adversity can become your sticky flypaper, miring you in agony.

In *Twenty-Four Hours a Day,* a compilation of daily readings from Alcoholics Anonymous literature, there is a meditation that reads in part: "It is not your circumstances that need altering, so much as yourself. After you have changed, conditions will naturally change."[7]

Clearly, the notion of a geographical cure for adversity is a delusion, but then all of us are delusional at one time or another. We need to minimize our delusions and maximize our consciousness as much as we can.

Leveraging your sweat equity built up through the mastering of earlier small and large adversities comes into play here, because you need that reservoir of *self-confidence* to know you can find a way through your latest troubles to reach your goal(s).

When you are ready to make a choice in confronting adversity, you'll find yourself struggling with choosing among many alternatives. The most important thing is to stop dithering by pretending to be *choosing* and begin *doing.* Doing calms the mind . . . and any action is better than no action at all.

Sadly, many people become mesmerized or frightened by the multitude of choices available to them. They believe they are "thinking before they leap." But they are really procrastinating . . . *dithering,* as I've said.

Adversity loves it when you're dithering. Like a dog, it instinctively senses uncertainty and knows that an equivocal master is no master at all.

Personally, I've never considered myself a philosophical thinker. By virtue of my personality and my education, I'm a pragmatist who is wired to get things done. Accordingly, it's my belief that too much thinking can actually get in the way of solving your problems and mastering your adversity.

If you find yourself paralyzed by indecision concerning what to do about your adversity, my advice to you is to move forward by *pretending* to be a dynamic pragmatist.

I've always found it ironic that while Shakespeare's character Hamlet is probably the world's foremost literary symbol of indecision, he knew the secret to transforming unwanted behavior traits and becoming forthright in one's intentions. In act III, scene 4, he advises his mother, Gertrude, whose behavior on a particular matter he wishes would change:

> Assume a virtue, if you have it not . . . For use almost can change the stamp of nature, and either curb the devil or throw him out with wondrous potency.[8]

In other words, do the right thing often enough—making a choice about confronting your adversity—and function will follow form; sooner or later your actions will become habit, and you will have transformed yourself into the decisive person you want to be. Making that first choice to confront your problems is also as deeply satisfying as it is empowering. You'll feel better knowing that you have taken control of your problem.

Remember, even if your choice turns out to be wrong, all that does is give you new, additional choices—for each is merely a fork we take on the road of life. Some of those forks are more productive than others, but as long as we keep moving ahead—and don't slump in surrender on the side of the road—new forks will continually be presented to us.

Keep choosing . . . keep moving . . . you can always change your course of action—*once you have a course of action.* The only mistake is to do nothing. Take action and see what happens five minutes or five months from now.

You might be wondering: *What about regret? I think it's my mistakes in life that have led me to my adversity. Now I'm afraid that I'll make things worse . . .*

The bottom line is that regret comes with the territory.

You will most definitely make mistakes, and you will regret them.

But so *what?*

AA taught me to seek out everyone I'd wronged and apologize to them. I have come to realize that the treasure in that step comes from the fact that when you make those amends you are ultimately apologizing to and forgiving *yourself.*

Handle your regret in the same way:

- Apologize to yourself for the mistakes you've made.

- Think about all you've learned from your experiences and how you can apply that learning (the sweat equity we've already discussed).

- Then move forward, taking the next fork in the road of life.

Don't let your mistakes collect and fester so they become like the chains of Marley's ghost. Remember the tempering process. It is your mistakes—and how you handle them—far more than your triumphs that make you who you are. I know for a fact that in my case, if I stripped away my mistakes, I wouldn't recognize myself.

You can escape the maelstrom of regret by sailing into the sheltered harbor of choices that are as wise as they can be at that moment. Don't worry about tomorrow. Concern yourself with discerning what seems to be the right thing to do *now,* and tomorrow will take care of itself.

Resist the siren call of the geographical cure. Whatever you do, don't try to run away! Stand your ground and confront your problems by remembering that:

- when it comes to adversity, there is no such thing as greener pastures.

- you must be both creative and patient to discover the multiple solutions that will unravel the knots of your adversity.

- mistakes are inseparable from life; how you handle the first determines how you will advance in the second.

In these ways, instead of running from adversity, you will move ever closer to mastering it, and be that much more at peace.

SEVEN

Four Techniques to Help You Harness the Power of Adversity

Mishaps are like knives that either serve us or cut
us, as we grasp them by the blade or the handle.

—*James Russell Lowell*

In the years following my heart attack, I knew I had to get a grip on my reactions to adversity in all its shapes or forms, or adversity would put me in my grave.

By now I'm certain you'd agree that learning how to harness adversity's power and transform it from an enemy to an ally is painstaking work. It involves not only becoming adept at a spate of physical and emotional disciplines, but also becoming familiar with the underlying spiritual and tangible practice of loving yourself and others.

Despite all the hard work it entails, mastering adversity can bring with it a state of being that approaches the mystical enlightenment talked about by Zen masters, some of whom I've quoted in previous pages.

Now I'd like to share with you my hard-won observations about harnessing the power of adversity through:

Attitude and the Mind—The power of positive imagery

Meditation: The Art of Letting Go—How doing nothing can be everything

Communication—Articulating the speech of the heart

Sharing, Not Managing—Not confusing the need to control with love

As I write about these disciplines that I deem absolutely essential for mastering adversity, my ideas, at first glance, might seem irrelevant to the pragmatic nuts and bolts business of resolving difficulties in your life. Trust me. These are the right skills for the job at hand.

Attitude and the Mind
The power of positive imagery

The number one factor in learning to deal with and ultimately master your adversity is your attitude. You need to change your perspective on how you approach your problems, and in that way reinforce your positive mindset.

Consider the opening words of Norman Vincent Peale's classic, *The Power of Positive Thinking:*

> Believe in yourself! Have faith in your abilities! Without a humble but reasonable confidence in your own powers you cannot be successful or happy. But with sound self-confidence you can succeed.[9]

Now compare the above quote to the beginning of this Alcoholics Anonymous *Meditation for the Day:*

> Be expectant. Constantly expect better things. Believe that what God has in store for you is better than anything you ever had before . . . A good life is a growing, expanding life, with ever-widening horizons, an ever-greater circle of friends and acquaintances and an ever-greater opportunity for usefulness.[10]

What both these passages allude to—as do myriad passages from other works of great wisdom—is the notion of living life with *enthusiasm.* (The word comes from the Greek term *enthusiasmos:* to be possessed by God.)

God, in this case, is not necessarily a white, male, father figure with a long beard. That may be who God is to you, and if so, that's fine, but substitute *Nature,* the *Cosmos,* or the *Force* for the word *God* and the substance of what I'm trying to say still comes across: thinking positively is paramount.

The mind, overwhelmed by fear, can be like a drop of mercury on a table, slithering and breaking into wildly evasive squirts and pieces. On the other hand, the mind, when positively rooted in a deep passion for life, is more certain and powerful than the forces that rotate the Earth. Once channeled toward a goal, the mind will cut its way to its destination like a river flows to the sea. Obstacles simply can't hold it up.

Overcoming adversity becomes inevitable when you avail yourself of the power of positive thinking—the power that enabled me to control my alcoholism, beat arthritis, and accomplish what was once considered impossible: total reversal of heart disease.

Long before the term *visualization* gained popularity, I would, in my mind's eye, journey the byways of my heart, following the strong flow of my blood. I continue to find this visualization exercise tremendously rewarding and still do it, reflecting along the way on the lifestyle changes that helped my heart to heal, and giving thanks to those who loved me enough to help me reach my state of vibrant wellness.

Ultimately, this entire book is about developing the wise—positive—attitude about adversity, which is essential to tapping adversity's power to enhance and improve your life.

Remember, when it comes to mastering adversity it's not:

"I *have* to do it" . . .

It's: "I have *it* to do."

If you can think that way, you're thinking positively, with the right imagery, and your battle is all but won.

Meditation: The Art of Letting Go
How doing nothing can be everything

Practicing meditation is the way to create and sustain your positive mindset. Most of the time, our heads are filled with an endless loop of the same thoughts formed over our lives. They drive us to distraction and often plunge us into anxiety. If we aren't doing something, then we are *thinking* about doing something. In the blur of this constant mental racket we lose our perspective of who we really are and our true place in the world . . .

Let's call that perspective our *center.*

Without our center—without *being centered*—we place an unhealthy emphasis on our goals and the adversity that prevents us from reaching them. And because a goal, by definition, is always *over there in the future,* our existence becomes obsessed with what's *going* to happen as opposed to what *is* happening.

It's like being lost in a dust storm. The turbulence created by our lack of center casts up clouds of dust that confuse us; we wander this way and that in our thoughts. Meditation allows us to escape the whirl-winds and dust of the preoccupied self and connect with the present moment—to be *mindful.* The clouds settle, and our way forward becomes clear to us.

In his marvelous book, *Wherever You Go, There You Are,* Jon Kabat-Zinn writes of the power of mindfulness:

> Mindfulness provides a simple but powerful route for getting ourselves unstuck, back into touch with our wisdom and vitality. It is a way to take charge of the direction and quality of our own lives, including our relationships within the family, our relationship to work and to the larger world and planet, and, most fundamentally, our relationship with our self as a person.[11]

One of the truest blessings of my adversity has been the rediscovery of what is important in life. I'm grateful that my problems caused me enough pain to stop me in my tracks and force me to confront what I was doing with my time on Earth. I realized I was wasting my time (because I wasn't *enjoying* my time), trying to live up to preconceived notions of where I was supposed to be in life, as opposed to savoring the present moment.

You already know that by trade, I am an industrialist who has spent my life and built my fortune in the realm of plastic caps and injection molding machines.

Accordingly, I will draw for you an analogy straight from the factory floor:

> *If we, for the moment, view ourselves as machines running through life, the power of adversity stems from its ability to radically readjust us by rounding our parts through its friction with the result of making us run more smoothly . . . Meditation provides the daily recalibration of that readjustment for optimum efficiency.*

Best of all, the benefits of meditation are freely available to all of us, regardless of our religious beliefs. Far from being a mystical art, meditation—at its core—is as down to earth and results-oriented as physical exercise.

There's lot of information available on different ways to meditate. Do a bit of web surfing or browse the shelves of your local bookstore to find a method that feels right for you. The bottom line is that you can meditate while you're walking your dog . . . behind the wheel commuting to work . . . playing golf . . . or playing the piano.

When *I* first tried to meditate I fell into the trap of trying to do it in the classic, Eastern way: sitting cross-legged, endlessly repeating a mantra . . . the whole Yogi/Swami/Zen Master nine yards.

What I didn't realize at the time was that the secret

to meditation is merely letting your mind go—not attempting to wrestle it into awkward contortions. My formal and mechanical meditation attempts were exactly in the wrong direction for me, which I discovered when I talked with Jon Kabat-Zinn, seeking his help in solving my apparent inability to meditate.

When Jon learned that I swam almost daily, he asked what I thought about during my laps in the pool. I told him I concentrated on my form and breathing. He said, "Al, you've been meditating for years, and you haven't recognized it. When you're in the pool you free your mind. That's all meditation is!"

Approach meditation like physical exercise, or even combine the two, like I do. The important thing is to meditate daily to rejuvenate and rebuild yourself, and to come to realize firsthand that adversity is just another name for the series of choices called life.

Communication
Articulating the speech of the heart

It was the poet W. B. Yeats who described prayer as the "inarticulate speech of the heart." Our goal is to articulate the heart's thoughts and feelings to others to help us see the way clear to mastering the power of adversity.

In my own journey I have come to understand that communication—open, guileless, risk-filled—has been the hardest attribute for me to develop. I still consider myself a novice communicator.

My rheumatoid arthritis shoved me stumbling along the first few steps of the communication path. Before that bout of suffering, I had barricaded myself off from the world.

Sure, I was interested in *manipulating* relationships using my positions of authority in life . . . I loved issuing orders . . . And I was a good boss (even in my love life), a caring and generous individual, as bosses go. But when it came to genuine communication of the sort that looks to *share* and not *control,* I was essentially clueless.

Today I believe this contributed greatly to making my first two marriages utter disasters. And then came Celia!

She revived in me the desire to communicate or, more to the point, to become communicatively *intimate.* But that initially just made my circumstances more difficult. *Wanting* something and knowing how to go about *achieving* it are two very different things.

While Celia instilled in me the craving for communicative intimacy, I was too locked away in my armor of perceived self-sufficiency to reach out to her. My ability to trust—critical to true communication and intimacy—did not exist.

The best I could do in those days was to articulate my needs and desires by the bland vocabulary of the world—providing my wife with material things while remaining emotionally and spiritually aloof.

Ironically, it took rheumatoid arthritis, which made me a physical cripple, to unshackle the wings of my spirit. As I struggled with the relentless pain, depression, and lack of certainty about the future, I was granted the gift of a lifetime: the opportunity to relearn trust.

I would never have accepted Celia's faithfulness, love, and devotion if not for my vulnerable state brought about by RA. Once I trusted a little, I was able to trust more and more, opening up to Celia, at first inarticulately with my heart and eventually with words of emotion and love openly expressed.

Gradually—and I am still learning—I came to understand that a great gift of adversity (if we choose to accept it) is coming to understand that we can only resolve our problems when we share our lives with others.

Being sullen and going about with the proverbial "chip" on one's shoulder—broadcasting *"you don't want to know what I'm about"* to the world—is the very antithesis to mastering the power of adversity.

Intimacy, on the other hand, is not a sign of weakness. It's a strength that flows from bringing yourself to communicate those thoughts and feelings that you've taught yourself not to share.

You simply must reach out to others. If you don't, you will never overcome adversity, any more than I could overcome being a drunk until I reached out in Alcoholics Anonymous.

It all comes back to tearing down those walls you've built around yourself with the bricks and mortar of your adversity. Find a chink in the wall and work at widening it. If you do, little by little the walls will crumble of their own accord.

Sharing, Not Managing
Don't confuse the need to control with love

The kind of communication I'm talking about stems from our primal yearning to *reveal, extend,* and *express* our innermost selves.

This is a far different paradigm than I had been operating from pre–rheumatoid arthritis. I was certainly accustomed to giving materialistically, but always with a catch: that I would remain emotionally off-limits.

During and after my RA, because of my illness, I began to change my mode of communication. Or, as I've said before, I used to love to manage Celia . . . then I managed to learn to love Celia.

I tried to stop acting like I knew what was best, even during those times when I actually may have. I tried hard to whittle from my communication attempts my facades of superiority and arrogance.

I made some progress, I think . . . And I might have remained on that plateau if not for the adversity of my heart disease.

As I've recounted, immediately after my heart attack,

the adversity sweat equity that I'd built up through my experience with rheumatoid arthritis came into play. Whereas before I would have retreated into myself (believing myself safer behind the walls of my adversity), I instead sought out my wife.

As Celia and I connected ever more deeply, the layers of my adversity peeled away like an onion, revealing choices and solutions that never would have been apparent to me on my own.

I tried then—and I'm still learning—to give up control . . . to constantly remind myself that when we fail to communicate our world is reduced, as if we were wearing blinders. This can lead to a tragic, downward cycle. We become more and more destructively self-involved, muttering to ourselves like prisoners driven mad by their long, solitary incarceration.

Only unfettered communication sets us free from this devolving spiritual and mental spiral, liberating us from adversity and giving us ideas on how to master it.

Some fortunate individuals are born with an open heart, able to freely and intimately communicate and thus forge strong links between themselves and the world. For the rest of us, the blessing of our adversity is that it can be the catalyst for changing our patterns of communication, transforming us for the better in profound ways.

EIGHT

Five Tips to Help You Put Adversity in Perspective

> If you want to forget all your other troubles, wear too tight shoes.
>
> —*The Houghton Line*

By now, hopefully, I've convinced you that adversity can be a friend and an ally. In this chapter, I give you some tips on how to take concrete steps to further put adversity in perspective, and help keep it working for you as opposed to against you:

- Have the right idea about money.
- Always get the facts.
- Think positively.
- Treat time as a resource.
- Give of yourself (time and money) to others less fortunate.

Have the Right Idea about Money—The desire for money brings with it impatience, which can turn one's existence into a living hell.

Like my grandfather and father, I craved success— power and money that could buy comfort and status. Maybe my obsession with material success has served me well. I really don't know.

What do you do with money? I am certain only that material success is meaningless without the human wealth that comes from joyous interaction with other people.

Money is particularly insidious, as it lulls us into a false sense of security. After all, you can only live in one house, drive one car, watch one TV, and so on. I always believed this to be a truism.

My cousin, British Methodist minister Reverend Leslie D. Weatherhead, wrote about the following dangers concerning making money:

> 1. *The danger of false security*—Money, especially if accompanied by health and happiness, can produce the illusion that it can buy anything and that all difficulties can be overcome by it. But it cannot. Rich people are certainly no happier than the poor. Generally the reverse.

> 2. *The danger of getting our sense of values wrong*—If we don't watch it, our money will warp our values. Hoarding gold . . . is harming us, if we are so obsessed by it that we no longer thrill to the golden glory of a cornfield, or the golden splendor of the setting sun . . .

3. *The danger of making us selfish*—You would think it would have the opposite effect: that a man would say when he had made a bit of money, "Now I can afford to be generous." But . . . in proportion to what they possess, the poor give more than the rich. Money makes you afraid you'll lose it. It makes you want to get just a bit more . . . It makes us look at ourselves with pathetic introspection and wonder whether we have made enough to keep us safe—in a world where there is no safety left, and no security save the love of God.[12]

It is fascinating to me that my cousin's words written over a half century ago still reverberate with truth.

1. How can you doubt that "rich people are generally no happier than the poor" when you read about the many celebrities, young and old, who find themselves in rehab due to alcoholism and substance abuse despite seeming to have it all?

2. Is there any question that our compulsion to "hoard gold" blinds us to all else when you see miserable souls chained to their Blackberries and laptops while vacationing with their families?

3. The fact that "the poor . . . give better than the rich" is indisputable, according to research by the NewTithing Group. In their report *The Generosity of Rich and Poor,* the group finds that "average middle class" and "middle rich" [income tax] filers donated a lower percentage of their

investment asset wealth to charity than did filers in any other tax filer category.[13]

This assertion is echoed by Arthur C. Brooks, author of *Who Really Cares: The Surprising Truth About Compassionate Conservatism,* who said in an interview on American Public Media's broadcast *Marketplace,* "When you look at charitable giving as a percentage of income, which is to say the sacrifice that people make, the most charitable people in America today are the working poor."[14]

Finally, in terms of money making us feel safe and secure, I can tell you from personal experience that when adversity calls, the most wealthy among us are those who have loving families and friends to fall back upon for support.

But you probably don't buy any of this—especially not if money is tight for you. I think I can hear you now: "Hell, if I had Al Weatherhead's dough I could be all touchy-feely, too, but I've got a mortgage payment to make, and my car needs new tires . . ."

Okay. I get it.

So here's my secret magic spell—one that will work better than three wishes from a genie to get you the material success you crave. I know this for a fact, because it worked for me.

You see, like a certain boy wizard, I too learned magic at a school to which I was sent when I was very young—eleven years old, to be exact. It was the University School, a private prep school founded in 1890 in Cleveland,

Ohio. I'll never forget the first time I saw the school's maroon and black crest, emblazoned with the motto:

RESPONSIBILITY LOYALTY CONSIDERATION

You'll notice that there is not a word about dollars. Just three tenets that I was taught to follow with the promise that, if I did, everything I desired in life would come to me.

At University School I was taught to take *responsibility* for myself and others. I remember how even the youngest boys took turns setting the lunch table and clearing the family-style meal while those older accepted responsibility for maintaining the school and its grounds.

I learned to be *loyal* to my family, friends, and the community, which naturally leads to *consideration* for others. Service to the larger community began in the earliest grades with food and clothing collections for the needy and broadened in scope as we boys grew older. Indeed, community service was a requirement for graduation.

Responsibility Loyalty Consideration . . . It was my misfortune to allow personal events in my life to blot the magic I'd learned at University School. My penance was the many years I spent traveling down bad roads paved with adversity—until I once again came to comprehend the powerful magic inherent in those three words. You might wish to replace those tenets with *Money, Power, Possessions* . . . but I am here to tell you from personal, painful experience that those things can disappear far more rapidly than they come.

Do this: for some finite period of time—three months, six months, a year—vow to make *Responsibility Loyalty Consideration* your guideposts for personal conduct. Ask yourself at every turn and before making any decision if you are taking into account these qualities. Be guided by these words in your business dealings . . . your personal relationships . . . and confronting your problems.

Then see what happens.

I know what happened for me. When I forgot what I'd learned at University School I became impoverished in every way you can imagine, and some you can't, unless you're a recovering alcoholic like I am.

But then I remembered the magic I'd learned at University School, and things changed for me, professionally and personally.

Learn from my mistakes—and your own. Follow my prescription, and your material success will come and adversity will fade, as if by magic.

Try it and see.

Always Get the Facts—Make sure to get the real facts, not those created by the imagination and fueled by anger, resentment, and bad memories.

Adversity and fear go hand in hand. And because of the overwhelming nature of fear, one of the greatest temptations in facing any kind of adversity is to remain ignorant and in denial. This may initially seem comforting, but it has the effect of lulling you into prolonged inaction. The longer you do nothing to confront your troubles, the more destructive they will be to you— becoming your master instead of the other way around.

What's required is to shine the bright light of your attention on your adversity . . . to poke and prod at it until you find the loose thread—the fact—with which to unravel it.

Take it from an old industrialist. Facts will always provide a solution to your adversity. The catch is that to *realize* those facts requires *deep attention.*

For example, at my factory, knowing that sales are down doesn't tell me anything about the problem I face. I need details. It's the same with adversity in every aspect of my life. When I had my heart attack, I remembered from my victory over rheumatoid arthritis that when it comes to illness (and truly, any form of adversity), *knowledge is power.*

I vowed to learn everything I could about the progress in the treatment of heart disease and spent hours every day poring over the most up-to-date information. With that knowledge filling my brain and Celia's love filling my heart, there was no way this disease was going to break my spirit.

An extra added benefit to always getting the facts is that you can't do so without engaging in communication—which in and of itself is a powerful tool to confronting and mastering the power of adversity.

At work you likely solve problems or move toward goals by communicating via emails and meetings. Try treating every problem—even the most personal—as if it were a business problem because, as I've already told you, every problem can be solved using the same process.

Take the problem we faced at Weatherchem concerning inventing and manufacturing the Flapper.

When Durkee asked me if there was a practical way to create a closure that had one side that could flap open, we started out by gathering the facts on what were the essentials to the companies that might buy our product and the consumers who would ultimately use it.

Granted, the facts can only take you so far. For example, in our decision to invest in creating the Flapper, we had no guarantee that Durkee would then give us the business, and while we knew there was a market, we didn't know how large it was.

A computer might have frozen due to the lack of such information. But you and I are not computers. We can gather enough facts to make a human leap of faith.

If you feel you've grown apart from somebody you care about, start the process of solving your issue with a session of facts gathering. You might ask the other party, "I don't feel good about us right now. Please tell me what you think."

Remember, facts are not necessarily truths. Facts sometimes reveal feelings. They also don't come in one great flood. They trickle in. But each fact gives you the opportunity to go forward in resolving the problem.

Conversely, all ignorance can do is amplify your fear. After my heart attack, for example, during an angiogram or some other unfamiliar medical procedure, my stress rocketed, and my mind whirled with deadly possibilities—all born out of ignorance.

As a currently card-carrying optimist, I never cease to be amazed by the quickness with which the mind latches onto the most morose scenarios. Rather than seeking facts—and usually the facts minimize rather than intensify fear—the mind prefers to remain in darkness and ignorance.

Gathering the facts will also help you to better understand others' points of view and enhance your overall comprehension of the adversity you face.

Remember:

- Ignorance invariably amplifies fear and despair.
- Knowledge always illuminates and enlightens.

Take the reins by becoming a private eye investigating the case of your adversity . . . Be the hero in your own mystery novel called *Your Life*.

Think Positively—Transform your adversity into your opportunity to triumph.

We've already touched upon the power of positive imagery. Here I want to focus on how important it is to make your subconscious mind work for you as opposed to against you.

During my battle with rheumatoid arthritis, I truly believe my recovery began when I was able to (unknowingly at the time) bring into play my subconscious. An example will suffice. Having read *The Arthritis Handbook* by Christiaan Barnard, I learned that 20 percent of RA sufferers totally recover. There are two ways for the mind to interpret that fact:

The positive: One in five completely recover. Super! *I'm going for it!*

The negative: Damn, 80 percent never completely recover. *I'm screwed.*

Apply this to how I might have contemplated my odds in recovering from alcoholism, a shattered career, a catastrophe of a personal life, and so on, and you'll see that attitude is everything when it comes to mastering adversity.

Please do not minimize the importance and relevance of what I'm telling you concerning positive thinking to help you master the power of adversity.

In business we have the 80/20 rule: you get 80 percent of your business from 20 percent of your customers. (This, incidentally, is called the Pareto Principle, named after the Italian economist who first recognized it in the early 1900s. It applies to many areas: 80 percent of contributions come from 20 percent of a charity's donors . . . 80 percent of computer software problems stem from 20 percent of programs . . . and so on.)

The 80/20 rule most definitely applies to positive thinking. Positive thinking may seem like it amounts to only 20 percent of the skill set you need to master adversity, but it will most certainly deliver 80 percent of your positive results.

Throughout my battle with RA, "one in five recover and that one is going to be *me*" became my catechism. You can think this way for yourself, whatever the problems you're facing. The first step to developing such a positive reference point is to focus not on your defeats but on what they've taught you and the opportunities they engender. Next, take *any improvement* in your situation—in the case of my RA, my ability to stand unsupported for a few seconds is an example—and celebrate it as a major victory, *because it is.*

Earlier in this book I shared with you how during my recovery from RA a miraculous turning point came the evening I held my hand before me and saw a sliver of light stream through my fingers from the streetlamp outside my kitchen window, light that a few months before never could have penetrated between my swollen fingers. You can just imagine what my subconscious did with that radiant sliver of light in terms of reinforcing my positive thinking.

Take *your* successes, no matter how small or seemingly trivial, and build upon them one after another, never looking back and never doubting that they are omens predicting that you will be the ultimate master of your adversity.

Treat Time as a Resource—Don't waste it feeling sorry for yourself.

We'll never have enough time. Paradoxically, understanding that concept allows us the potential to enjoy the time we have. As Arnold Bennett writes in *How to Live on 24 Hours a Day:*

> Time is the inexplicable raw material of everything. With it, all is possible; without it, nothing. The supply of time is truly a daily miracle, an affair genuinely astonishing when one examines it.
>
> You wake up in the morning, and lo! Your purse is magically filled with twenty-four hours of the unmanufactured tissue of the universe of your life! It is yours. It is the most precious of possessions . . . No one can take it from you. It is unstealable. And no one receives either more or less than you receive.
>
> In the realms of time there is no aristocracy of

wealth, and no aristocracy of intellect. Genius is never rewarded by even an extra hour a day. And there is no punishment. Waste your infinitely precious commodity as much as you will, and the supply will never be withheld from you . . . Moreover, you cannot draw on the future. Impossible to get into debt! You can only waste the passing moment. You cannot waste tomorrow; it is kept for you. You cannot waste the next hour; it is kept for you . . .

You have to live on this twenty-four hours of daily time. Out of it you have to spin health, pleasure, money, content, respect, and the evolution of your mortal soul. Its right use, its most effective use, is a matter of the highest urgency and of the most thrilling actuality. All depends on that. Your happiness—the elusive prize that you are all clutching for, my friends—depends on that . . .

We shall never have any more time. We have, and we have always had, all the time there is.[15]

Each moment of time approaches us with infinite possibility, summoning us to compassion, understanding, and wellbeing. Can you—*will you*—open yourself to the potential of the moment?

I implore you not to miss the show that time is putting on for you. Don't let problems pollute your every twenty-four-hour cup of life.

Time, after all, is the only resource you have to expend against adversity. (Even if you throw money at a problem, for instance, all you're really doing is buying yourself time saved by having others tackle whatever it is that's troubling you.)

We each have some recreation we enjoy doing "to pass the time." I like to swim. You may enjoy playing golf or tennis . . . bowling . . . or saving the world from aliens playing a video game. In all these activities we instinctively understand that, win, lose, or draw, playing the game is where the real fun is. Our time spent in *doing* whatever it is we like to do pleasures us in myriad ways.

What would happen, do you think, if you *approached your adversity* as if it were a rather difficult shot on the seventeenth hole? Or a particularly adept tennis opponent? Do you think you could "pass the time" tinkering with how you are going to solve your adversity the way you might tinker with your golf swing?

Let me put it another way. Do you think you could take the mindset and skill sets you've developed through time and put them to work against the adversity you're confronting? The same way you might, let's say, apply your accumulated tennis ability to improving your game?

Is it worth *trying?*

Remember, all problems are solved the same way. Granted, there is an immense difference in intensity in putting together a jigsaw puzzle compared to putting together a shattered life—but ultimately both are put together in the process of trial and error over *time.*

I'll end this section with two last bits of advice:

• No matter how tough your day has been, always go to bed believing that your cup of time will be refilled tonight.

• Whatever you want to do with your time—including wasting it—is okay, as long as you're enjoying yourself.

Give of Yourself (Time and Money) to Others Less Fortunate—Put the adversity you are experiencing in perspective by familiarizing yourself with the adversity that others are experiencing.

Acts of charity should come with a warning label: *Caution: giving is addictive.*

After my heart attack, I found myself pursuing the riches of the spirit. *Money can't buy happiness* may seem like a trite cliché, but the fact remains that there really are only *three* things you can do with money: spend it, give it away, or pay taxes.

I draw your attention to the epigraph of this book by Edward Courtenay:

"What wee gave, wee have;

What wee spent, wee had;

What wee left, wee lost."

Those words were written a very long time ago, but they are indeed timeless.

"What wee gave, wee have"—As I've previously discussed, giving is truly the most *self*-ish act of all, because of generosity's tempering process and the simple fact that nothing makes you feel better than to give. It's also the quickest way to escape from the syndrome of viewing yourself as being at the center of the universe because it takes you out of yourself while providing you with a concrete way to change the world.

"What wee spent, wee had"—A lot of us compulsively shop in a desperate attempt to distract ourselves from our perceived problems. We're like alcoholics with their bottles or junkies taking their next fix; our new TV, car, outfit, or whatever might make us feel better for a little while, but the high soon wears off, and we're back where we started, except for being that much poorer. That being said, at least we have *something* to show in exchange for the money we had.

"What wee left, wee lost"—When my father passed away, I heard somebody say, "They should have bought another casket to bury his money." That remark was cruel, crass, heartless—and absolutely *true* in the sense that wealth left behind may be of benefit to one's heirs, but like they say, "You can't take it with you . . ."

Beyond the acquisition of necessities, the true value of money is in its potential to reveal to us the *real* purpose of life: to experience and demonstrate love.

Although I had always considered myself to be compassionate in terms of contributing to charities, before my heart attack, I had never been good at outwardly expressing love. I was, after all, the son of a man who could hug me only when he was drunk. I also grew up in an era when men were not expected to wear their hearts on their sleeves. Expressions of love were equated with weakness and dependence, which were the antonyms of a real man.

But my heart attack turned me into an enthusiastic hugger.

I have been known to hug for any reason—just like I used to be when it came for an excuse to have a drink.

The setting sun deserves a hug.

On the sidewalk I will give you a hug that is hard enough to make you catch your breath.

A hug at any moment for any reason is wonderful, and I believe that no matter what their reaction or expression, people really *love* to be hugged.

An act of charity is *another kind of hug.*

It's also really an act of love—*a loving hug from afar.*

As I've mentioned, I have made some substantial charitable gifts through my involvement with my family foundation. Today, the Weatherhead Center for International Affairs at Harvard University, the Weatherhead East Asian Institute at Columbia University, the Weatherhead School of Management at Case Western University, and the Weatherhead PET Center for Preventing and Reversing Heart Atherosclerosis at the University of Texas-Houston are some of our foundation's philanthropic endeavors.

Why am I telling you this? What are you supposed to garner from this list of major charitable endowments I have been fortunate enough to make?

Remember, this is a *self-help* book. We are not primarily concerned with how your giving can help *others,* but, rather, how your acts of giving can benefit *you* in relation to overcoming adversity.

So here's the point I'm trying to make:

I give . . . The rest of the sentence is not important. *How much* you give is far less important than the mindset you have when you make the gift.

Perhaps no parable better illustrates this point than the Widow's Mites, a beautiful story from the Bible about how Jesus watched the rich cast their gifts into the Temple basket. The rich men all put in bulging sacks of gold. Then Jesus saw a poor widow put in just two meager coins, called "mites" in those days. Jesus then said to his disciples, "Truly, I say to you that this poor widow has cast in more than all the others." In other words, that widow gave everything she had, while those rich guys weren't going to miss their donations. So who cared more about improving the world?

Jesus, you see, understood that it is the *intention* of the charitable gift far more than its *size* that can transform ourselves and thus transform the world.

Perhaps this is also what Jesus was getting at when he said, in Matthew 19:23, "Truly I say to you, it is hard for a rich man to enter the kingdom of heaven."

I think he meant that it can be more difficult for those who are wealthy to avail themselves of the *self*-ish personal healing power of giving, ironically, because it can be easier for them to give money and thus avoid rolling up their sleeves and getting personally involved, that is, giving of themselves.

Now you may have your own ideas about "the kingdom of heaven." For me, it is here on Earth, and I reside in it because of the wonderful way I feel when I give from my heart as opposed to my wallet: whether my gift is $5 million to a university or $5 to some individual in desperate need I come across on the sidewalk.

I came around to this way of thinking as the Weatherhead Foundation evolved from being a passive contributor to projects, with little or no input into the design or management of the programs being funded, to a philanthropic organization fueled by creative involvement.

In 1979, my brother Dick and I made some critical decisions for the foundation that drastically altered how and why we provide funds. The result of those decisions repositioned the Weatherhead Foundation as an organization that would always be intertwined at every level with the causes and projects we foster.

If *you* want to get the utmost from your charitable giving in terms of garnering a new perspective on your adversity, be like me with my foundation, and give of *yourself* instead of merely giving *money*.

I've moved far beyond this form of "checkbook philanthropy."

So can you.

Sure, it's nice to send a check to the Cancer Society, but the high is fleeting. The act of writing that check gets lost among all the other checks you're writing to pay your bills.

You're helping the cause to which you're contributing, but you're missing out on helping yourself.

You'll get much more out of giving by going to the hospital for half a day and volunteering to read to patients. Maybe that hospital visit . . . time spent mentoring a parentless, disadvantaged child . . . or working for a couple of hours in the kitchen at a homeless shelter . . . will inspire you to tackle your problems in a new way or even show you that your problems, which you thought were insurmountable, are really not that terrible after all.

You might even get more than you give in terms of receiving a vivid lesson on how others have learned to master the power of adversity.

Try giving one to one in this way, and you will be amazed at the profound difference it will make in the way you feel about yourself, the world, and your problems.

When it comes to giving, I don't pity those in need. I don't have sympathy for them. Yes, my alcoholism has put me on comparable paths with substance abusers I have come across, but my years in AA have taught me that no two sets of circumstances are alike. Anyway, to pity and sympathize are outward acts. These reactions don't truly resonate inside. *Only love does.*

The rewards of charitable acts of love are profound, beginning with the way to tame your adversity by putting it in perspective as compared to the circumstances of others in need—be they on the other side of the tracks or on the other side of the world.

Next, giving casts a glow that you can use to illuminate your way out of your own personal darkness. Please allow me to share with you a personal fact or two, to help you to understand what I'm telling you.

In 1979, Celia and I lost a child to a miscarriage. Celia desperately wanted to be a mother. I now say with deep regret and sorrow that my desire did not equal hers. I had children from previous marriages. Celia, however, persisted, though obstacles blocked the path to her heartfelt desire. At that time I was still in the crippling throes of rheumatoid arthritis, and the drugs I was taking for RA could have worked against the possibility of pregnancy. Needless to say, we were both suffering traumatically due to this awful adversity. For nearly two years, Celia's life alternated between despondency and hope, but in the end, the baby was not to be.

It was then that Celia went from being an unofficial philanthropic advisor as my spouse to formally joining the board of trustees of the Weatherhead Foundation.

She shone almost immediately as a challenger, ever looking for ways in which the foundation could raise its sights ever higher and become even more creative in its giving. Perhaps Celia was rechanneling her powerful maternal instincts to this new endeavor, for as we emerged from the adversities of my arthritis and Celia's disappointment at not having a child, the foundation began to play a more central role in each of our lives. I guess you could say it became our baby . . . and it was helping us to become *self*-ish in our acts of philanthropy.

Choosing to fund projects actively instead of passively proved to be challenging, frustrating, draining, stimulating, and, most of all, joyful work. It provided Celia and, by extension, me, with *good* problems . . . adversity that was *fun* . . . and so taught us more about how to tackle adversity that was not so pleasant.

Today, Celia sometimes refers to the Weatherhead Foundation as the offspring of our love. She feels toward it like a parent feels toward a child.

You don't need to start a foundation to profit from this wonderful way to handle adversity and put it in perspective. Volunteer for a committee at your club or place of worship . . . coach a Little League team . . . be a Big Brother or Big Sister . . . help cook a meal at a shelter . . . Your choices and opportunities are endless for getting involved and giving of yourself, as opposed to only giving from your wallet.

That's not to say that you are obligated to act on every opportunity presented to you to help. You don't have to volunteer your life away. Just do what you think you can.

I've given money to the Rosary Hall Alcohol Rehabilitation Center in Cleveland, but far more meaningful to me in terms of gaining perspective on my adversity is the time I've spent there visiting those who are starting on the sober path that I currently walk. The act of love inherent in overcoming my inertia and separation from the world and visiting people who are currently where I've been strengthens me as much—or even more—than it strengthens them.

During such visits I feel a surge of euphoria.

I feel *blessed*.

What can a few problems be to you if you're blessed?

As Celia and I along with others have sought to advance and evolve the Weatherhead Foundation, we have—through pure luck and hard work—settled into a variety of philanthropic endeavors in addition to the ones previously mentioned. Each is branded in unique ways with our style of hands-on, active management giving, but yet each is as different from one another as offspring will always be.

Truly they reflect the loves of our lives: management, peace, and health. And yes, they are also the blossoms of adversity: the byproducts of hearts that have endured suffering and, having suffered, learned anew what it means to fall passionately in love with life.

Our family foundation is not about titles, egos, or having my name plastered on buildings. It has everything to do with human-to-human interaction, much like the healthy interaction of loving parents and children, for the betterment of humankind.

Remember, you don't need a foundation to give in the same manner and realize the same benefits for yourself . . .

All it takes—no matter how much or how little you give—is to develop a deep and meaningful relationship with the charity or cause you choose to support.

$5 or $5 million . . . the littlest change for the better or worse in the world is just as important at the most massive one. As the phrase that encapsulates the substance of science's chaos theory so aptly puts it: *the flapping of a butterfly's wings in China can amplify into a tornado in Kansas* . . .

Before you right now is the opportunity to put your problems in perspective and thus transform *your* world—as well as *the* world—by giving of yourself to others.

If you don't believe giving is the greatest high there is, try it for a while and see how you feel: if you begin to feel better about yourself and your adversity, then my advice has helped you.

That is my act of love—my hug from afar—for *you*,

which will help *me* in mastering, and thus leveraging, the power of *my* next adversity.

See how it works?

NINE

Problem Solving Is One of the Great Joys in Life

Smooth seas do not make skillful sailors.

—African proverb

Harnessing with relentless passion the infinite power of adversity has led me to stunning revelations. Before adversity struck, I was preoccupied with false impressions of personal appearance and grandiosity. Adversity beat out of me self-delusion and stripped me of false vanities. And as I began to understand my own suffering, I began to view life with new eyes.

For example, I came to see that Weatherchem, my plastic cap and closure company, was alive. It is not merely a place built of concrete, steel, machinery, and motion, but a living, breathing entity pulsating with energy and in possession of a soul. When I am in my factory and listening closely, I can hear its heartbeat, and not just in the rhythms of its machinery but individually and collectively from the people who work within its walls.

I have also come to believe that successful management is more like taking a pulse than taking inventory. After decades of leadership experience, I can now walk onto any factory floor and intuit its health from the spark, rhythm, and air of its space.

Is there the buzz of dissonance or the hum of synchronicity?

Confusion or creativity?

Chaos or vision?

Conflict or unity?

In short, is the adversity that inevitably must run through a factory like electricity, a *friction* or a *fuel*?

I can always find the answers to those questions in the faces of the employees, for beyond all the mechanics of the place there is one truth: a factory is a collective human endeavor. Indeed, much of what is wrong in a good deal of current business theory and practice is its failure to recognize that the heart of any factory beats to the rhythms of its employees.

The bottom line must not be profit, because profit can only come as a fruit of the health and dreams of the human endeavor the factory represents. Management's responsibility, then, is to cultivate within the workplace

But 1
my nev
heights
On 1
where.
self-ima
the prir
free to r
creating
a salary
invoices
a stickii

Adve
ask que
way to

One
Ankney
which t
footage.
the pipi
had at th
saved pi

We s
color the
dried cc
than a ye
for, and
wood w

an environment that lends itself to creativity, dreams, and a collective spirit larger than the sum of its paychecks and mechanical parts.

I have learned all this—as I've learned most everything else—through adversity's hard knocks. As a child, dreaming in my father's factory, I saw the camaraderie, respect, love, and energy shared by Weatherhead employees. I watched, too, as my parents poured their lives into the company. All this created the heartbeat of that factory.

Then, with the death of my father, the Weatherhead Company developed a diseased heart. Mismanagement crushed the human endeavor upon which the factory thrived, as you and I thrive on clean air, water, nourishing food, a healthy heart, and a happy soul.

Some would say the business simply failed. To me, the demise of my father's company was a death in the family. This adversity left me reeling. It took a long time for me to realize that my failure to be the heir to my father's company, prestige, and fortune was really a blessing, a gift from God to me. As adversity forced me to wrestle with ruined hopes and scorched self-images, I used the techniques I have shared with you in this book to transform as with an alchemist's craft the dull lead of adversity into glittering success.

Adversity empowered me to realize that what was torn down, I could—and needed—to rebuild. And so I decided to start my own company. For several years I put out

feelers
were t
about
    Th
piece
and R
named
sell th
viousl
his fac
    Sui
young-
demar
potent
    I w
tant, a
only p
Curio
you'd
    An
under:
diseng
    A fe
about
on Dec
promi
busine
size cc

I could share with you hundreds of similar stories. There were many triumphs and not a few failures. But as my leadership matured and my creativity blossomed, I came to see failure not as a defeat but as learning one more way that something is *not* done. Such learning can be daunting, but it is the only way a business can survive and thrive.

Mechanics are the easy part. Remember, always and in all ways, a factory is a living, breathing organism. Human elements are the challenge.

At one of our first staff meetings we discussed company benefits. As we knocked around ideas to promote productivity, commitment, and creativity, the plant controller asked, "Why bother? People are like cattle. You can herd them any way you want."

I fired him. Of the original employees, he was the only one who did not stay.

From that day forward, I made sure everyone at Weatherchem understood my lifelong fundamental conviction: everyone deserves to be loved, respected, and honored.

In all these ways, old machinery molted into new technology, and where others saw the drag of employee overhead, I imagined a profit-sharing plan.

The start of Weatherchem coincided with the beginning of my marriage to Celia. And I am ashamed to tell you that I could apply none of what I was learning about mastering adversity in a professional guise to the plane wreck of my personal life.

I remember distinctly how Celia and I were still honeymooners in Florida when I let it slip that I'd had my—now our—house in Cleveland carpeted without consulting her. In retrospect, I understand why she was hurt and disappointed; this was to be *our* home, and she was looking forward to creating a warm and loving environment. At the time, however, I only felt challenged and dismissive of her pain. You see, as I was used to making decisions in my factory, I presumed to make them in my marriage as well.

I did not then know enough about conquering adversity to ask concerning my marriage the same questions I asked myself at work: *Why* am I doing things this way? Was there a *better* way?

I suppose I thought that such questions belonged in the vocabulary of entrepreneurs, but not a newlywed husband with steel wrapped around his heart.

My life, then, was a paradox, although I could not see it at the time. On one hand, adversity had taught me how to rebuild my confidence and redefine success—both of which I was doing remarkably well via my new business. I patted myself on the back for not being a Scrooge to my employees. I convinced myself that I was a warm and compassionate individual because I was so concerned with their welfare, providing my workers with state-of-the-art benefits—from healthy lifestyle incentives to profit-sharing retirement plans.

Professionally, I truly was *not* driven by the idea that *I* needed to succeed, but that my *factory*—the breathing, living organism—had to. In these ways I felt safe that in my professional life I had begun to master adversity.

But I now realize that in my personal life—as I started my new marriage—adversity had beaten me. My bitterness over my previous marriages had caused me to shut down emotionally. Adversity conned me into believing that in the inevitable give-and-take between spouses, I was better off taking with hardly any giving.

Thus, adversity did to me what it always does to us if left uncontested: it bred fear, isolation, and emotional and physical paralysis. The attributes that I used as a successful businessperson—to accurately judge and take a risk, forthrightly communicate, and be willing to do the dirty work—I simply could not imagine applying in my marriage.

Instead, I tried to control every facet of our lives together once Celia and I came to Cleveland. I picked out her clothes and chose her car; I doled out an allowance for her to run the house. I suppose in a strange and twisted way, I was showing what I thought to be love. I realize now that I was unconsciously emulating my father's behavior, which was to be controlling—as a substitute for loving—to keep Celia at bay. I didn't understand then—and probably could not have understood—that controlling love, no matter its intentions, suffocates rather than nurtures.

It may seem incredible to you that I viewed my factory as a living, breathing organism, but could only see my marriage as an opportunity for me to pull a stone-cold powerplay.

It seems incredible to me, in retrospect . . .

Positive change came slowly, largely through the transforming power of Celia's persistent love. Patiently she knocked tiny chinks in my heart's armor—never quite enough to break through, but fortunately for me, just enough for her to glimpse inside and wonder, *what if?*

As I've already shared with you, despite all of Celia's valiant determination and a decade of our marriage, it took my crippling and humbling by rheumatoid arthritis to give me the slap I needed to shatter all my barricades and guide me to a true mastering of adversity in my personal life. And so for me, adversity has been a blessed enemy, indeed.

If you've read this far, you know that I believe that problem solving—moving from challenge to challenge, no matter how painful and difficult—is the greatest thrill in the world. However, I wouldn't want to leave you with the false impression that I'm incapable of backsliding once in a while.

In the early 1970s, my hunger to make money and

acquire the power I believed it automatically bestowed still tortured me on occasion. Blinded by frustration due to Weatherchem's "sloth-like" growth, I stormed into the office of James Sheedy, a company director, to announce that I was selling the place, period.

Sheedy listened patiently as I spouted off. When I ran out of steam he replied, "Al, you're not going to sell your company. Weatherchem is the closest thing on this planet to being pure *you*."

With that single sentence my friend put me in my place and straightened me out by reminding me of the fathomless rewards my company offered me: an outlet for my creativity and a chance to build a successful business to my benefit and to the benefit of my employees and customers—and even to your benefit, if you've availed yourself of the convenience afforded by my company's closures on just about any product you may use.

The lesson here: be especially appreciative of loved ones and friends who are ready, willing, and able to call your bluff and tell you that you're full of crap when the occasion warrants.

Only I know best is a terrible mindset for confronting adversity. By discouraging communication it builds walls in the blink of an eye. Once you've locked yourself in, it's like being in solitary confinement: you are as lonely as you are imprisoned within your own perceived limitations and prejudices.

It's far better to collaborate. Today I prefer to plant seeds in others' minds while they plant seeds in mine. Some germinate and some don't. But those that do tend to sprout and bloom in, for me, unimaginable and wonderful ways.

I remember as a young man riding my quarterhorse near my dad's ranch in the Santa Rita Mountains of southern Arizona. In that part of the country there are towering peaks and deep canyons, with crevices in the rock walls. I enjoyed seeing how far I could squeeze through those narrow chinks in the rock before I could go no farther and I'd have to back carefully out. I thought at the time I was exploring new and wonderful things, but was I really?

Our own narrow-mindedness can confine us as much as those chasms did me as a young man. On your own, your path is constrained by towering, narrow canyons of your own creation. You *think* you're going somewhere *new*, but in reality you're going *nowhere you haven't been before*.

View solving your own problems as a collaborative effort—and discover how the benefits of communication that such collaboration requires can make not just the positive outcome but the ongoing process of confronting adversity so deeply satisfying.

After all, your problems will always involve other people—unless you are a castaway on a Godforsaken island. So take advantage of others' creativity. Let the lessons adversity has to teach you about collaboration through communication help you revitalize your personal and professional life, and in the process, redefine for you—as it has for me—the true meaning of success.

As I write this, I have recently returned from a visit to my factory, where I had a hug for everyone and everyone had a hug for me.

I ran into Victor, a new employee who came to us after being laid off by Ford.

"I like this place," Victor told me. "People are happy."

"I know," I said, and hugged him one more time. "I want to be here for another twenty-five years."

"You'll be here, Al," Victor grinned. "One way or another. You'll be here."

I will always believe that problem solving—moving from mystery to mystery and challenge to challenge— is the greatest thrill in the world. And I will always believe that the stimulation and engagement of the mind is our true calling as human beings.

You already know that your true question in life should be "Why *not* me?"

From there, it's just a short leap to "For what reason am I here on Earth?"

I believe that last question will bring you around to embracing your adversity . . . pointing the way to your greater purpose . . . and connecting you with a grander, and yes, even divine, plan.

I'm here to help you along the way.

One way or another, I'll be here . . .

TEN

There Is Always a Great Idea Lurking in Adversity . . . Will You Find It?

I had a lover's quarrel with the world.

—Robert Frost

What propelled me through the adversities of pain, depression, loneliness, and desperation afflicting me in my life?

Why is it that some people placed in similar devastating straits make it through with important lessons learned, as I did, while some seem to stumble completely, losing their grip on life?

Even today, I'm not certain why I'm a survivor. Some of it was diligence of human spirit, I guess, and some resourcefulness of body and mind.

I do know that while I experienced some horrible reversals of fortune, I also benefited from luck: without Celia I never would have made it this far, let alone have advice on mastering the power of adversity to share with you.

And this much more I know: making a path through adversity involves many choices.

In my own family, I have seen adversity envelop my siblings in darkness . . .

David, my brother born three years after me, chose to run from adversity. He left home when he was eighteen and moved to Essex, Connecticut, a seaport on the Connecticut River, where he took a minimum-wage job in a paint company and pursued his love of sailing. David wanted to escape the driving expectations of our strong-willed father who insisted he go to college and make something of himself. I, too, pleaded with David to go to college, which he finally decided to do in 1951, ultimately graduating from Boston University.

College, however, did not change David's direction. Just like me, early in life, he drifted from one dead-end job to another. And just like me, he drank. He had his Weatherhead inheritance to fall back on and ended up in Boston. He was gay and found a loving relationship with a long-term companion, but in every other aspect he merely continued to muddle along, settling instead of aspiring.

Shortly after our father's death, David attempted suicide with booze and barbiturates. We got him into McLean Hospital, and because I was a recovering alcoholic thanks to AA, I was able to touch his heart and soul in his own fight with his demons. David stayed at McLean for many months.

After his release, he returned to Boston, where he tried to find some happiness in his old passion of sailing, but now the sea frightened him. He began wearing suits, smoking a pipe, and mimicking from memory many of our father's poses. He resumed his alcoholism for solace and to hide from the world; he left life. David's life played out dismally, to our sad loss. He died of esophageal and laryngeal cancer in 1984 at the age of fifty-six.

The more David ran from adversity, the tighter it clung to him and the greater the pain it caused him.

Let me tell you something about my brother Richard Weatherhead and his work as the initial guiding light of the Weatherhead Foundation during the period immediately following our father's death. Dick was my baby brother—nine years younger. Like David and I, he loved our father but was at times intimidated and infuriated by him. And like us, he found his methods of dealing; one was drinking, and the other was overwhelming dear old dad with brain power. Describing Dick as brilliant would be a serious understatement. He was on the Dean's List through his whole time at Harvard and received his master's and doctorate in philosophy from Columbia University, where he became a tenured professor. Dick was also a successful author, his books covering a broad range of subjects on Latin America. To deepen his knowledge of the Spanish language, he translated Shakespeare from English to Spanish, and when he became immersed in Japan he became fluent in Japanese also. Dick also took the lead in handling the Weatherhead Foundation after our father's death. In short, his mind, when occupied, was a whirlwind of brilliant energy and productivity.

Dick, it turned out, was also gay. As I did with David, I reassured him that his sexual proclivity would never affect our relationship. Dick lived with a Japanese man, also a professor, and the four of us—Dick and his partner, Celia and I—enjoyed each other's company with love, laughter, and conviviality.

Yet, for reasons mysterious to me even now, Dick began to slip away. In retrospect, I believe his adversity began, paradoxically, with financial prosperity (which goes to show you that adversity can take many guises). He'd been used to scrimping by on his professor's salary, but when he began receiving Weatherhead Company dividends his income ballooned.

The money turned out to be a cruel disappointment, however, because it arrived almost in concert with a diagnosis of severe heart disease in 1979, when he was only forty-five. His health preoccupied him. He was haunted with visions of his own death. He lost interest in his work, escaping more and more into the bottle. His money provided escape for a little while as he and his companion traveled the world, but soon, even that came to be for him a meaningless drudgery.

October 1987 was the last time I saw him. I remember him standing in the doorway of his Manhattan apartment, a wide smile on his face as he reassured me he was fine.

As a recovering alcoholic, I could spot his lies miles away. I could see then that he couldn't wait for me to go so he could retreat into an alcoholic haze. By Thanksgiving he was dead at the age of fifty-three.

We three were brothers. Only one of us made it out of the maelstrom of adversity:

Slaying dragons of depression . . .

Exchanging emotional frigidity for emotional love . . .

Recovering from alcoholism that has swept through our generations, sucking so many of my family into inescapable black holes.

As I think of my brothers I feel love and deep, wistful sadness that adversity mastered them, instead of the other way around. I am brokenhearted that I could not share with my brothers the experiences of my own journey to confront and harness the power of adversity.

I am grateful and thankful for the opportunity to share these experiences and lessons with *you.*

Now I have a few last words to offer you . . .

Pay the deepest attention to the freeing ideas and thoughts lurking among the dark shadows of adversity. There you will find the compass that will unfailingly guide you to *what* you want, *how* you feel, and *how far* you will go to achieve your goals.

Conversely, if you don't seek to find its deeper meaning, adversity will drive you farther into the darkness, erecting wall upon wall of fear, distrust, anger, apathy, and suspicion to cut you off from people and the world. Adversity truly is two-edged. Left to its own devices it creates walls. When properly channeled and directed, it splinters them.

Yes, climbing into the arena to master your adversity must inevitably involve pain and risk. You will be required to discard whatever is false in your life. But the reward is freedom.

So climb your mountain. The view will be worth it. Freed from your walls, your vistas will be breathtaking and infinitely changing.

At my age, you would probably forgive me if I chose to spend my time reminiscing about the past . . . If I lost myself in happy, misty reveries of days spent with old and dear friends . . .

But for me, that could never be.

I relish the present moment and planning for the future.

Nearly forty years ago I started my company with faith, trust, enthusiasm, energy—and with one product for two customers. At Weatherchem we always believed in ourselves and our products, and always—*always*—believed in taking care of our customers. The results speak for themselves, and today I still revel in going to work each day in the best plastics closure company in America!

That same kind of enthusiasm buoys me along the river of life with its inevitable daily surprises—good and bad . . .

I may chat with a plant worker and feel the surge of human connection . . .

Open a letter from one of the causes to which I contribute, experience the sweetness of knowing that I am making a positive difference in the world, and long to do more . . .

Swim laps in a pool, scudding through the water like a cloud through the blue sky as I meditate on the miracle and mantra of my breathing . . .

And end each day talking with my beloved Celia, exchanging words and touches, sharing all that has passed between us and anticipating all that is yet to come . . .

All these great old and new joys I owe to my blessed enemy, adversity.

My life is not perfect. No life can be. Adversity still haunts and taunts me.

But I will *never* let it suck me back into the shadows.

Instead, I will continue to grow by taking advantage of all the new opportunities presented to me by my own, personal unending stream—and *infinite bounty*—of adversity.

You, too, can discover the powerful and liberating ideas lurking in the dark shadows of your blessed adversity.

Just remember that:

- **Adversity is all powerful**—it either creates misery or destroys it.

- **Adversity will always hurt**—it is up to us to transform that hurt into limitless freedom and positive transformation.

- **Adversity is the bridge that can carry us to our future**—it will take us to where we can live fully, bravely, and meaningfully in the world.

I hope and pray that you and I will continue our learning together for our own benefit and that of our families, friends, and humankind. The heat of our tempering adversity will cast the glow that illuminates the path.

For what more could we ask?

AFTERWORD

I wish you all imaginable success and happiness. Live in the future, manage change. It starts with you.

You are invited to share your experiences and thoughts on my website. While I can't promise to personally reply to each of you, I'll do my best to keep up with you.

www.powerofadversity.net

APPENDIX A

Adversity Check List

Here I've condensed my list of rules for mastering adversity for easy review and to assist you in using the accompanying Adversity Work Sheet. Please refer to the page numbers for elaboration on these important rules.

1. We're not meant to be happy . . . we're meant to grow.   6

Adversity acts like a grain of sand inside an oyster; it is the irritant in our lives that can stimulate us to create pearls.

2. Positive thinking is imperative.   21, 87, 106

Positive thinking can change your life and, in the process, give your life back to you. It can help to heal you physically and put you on the path to heal your spirit.

3. You are not at the center of the universe.

22, 45

Your place in the universe has nothing to do with your achievements, pride, or real or imagined sins, but with your ability to harness the power of adversity to learn how to react—and how not to react—to life's troubles.

4. Instead of "Why *me?* . . . Why *not* me?"

34, 49

The question that we must ask ourselves can only sensibly be "Why not me?" when we rid ourselves of the debilitating anger that comes from our sense of being singled out by adversity.

5. It is luckier to *earn* than to *receive.*

35–36

The rewards of work are far sweeter than those bestowed on us by fortune . . . and you can't earn by work without adversity.

6. Be *self*-ish and put yourself *first,* by putting yourself *last.*

40, 49

Fight the primitive "me first" impulse that many of us experience confronting adversities and help short-circuit your stress and anger.

7. Never think "I *have* to do it."   **46**
   Instead, think "I have *it* to do."
   Mastering adversity is all about
   choice. First you choose to do it . . .
   and you continue to do it by continuing your series of choices.

8. I *suffer* passes . . . I *suffered* never
   passes . . . A blade remains
   tempered long after the fire that
   scorched it has faded away.   **51**
   Mind, body, and spirit forged
   in the furnace of adversity builds
   day by day, just like physical
   strength through exercise.

9. Cultivate the *self*-ish virtues of
   modesty, gratitude, courtesy,
   self-control, compassion, perse-
   verance, and indomitable spirit.   **56–61**
   Use them to confront and con-
   quer your bitterness and anger
   when adversity rears its ugly head.

10. Adversity creates walls . . . When
   you tear down those walls you
   create spectacular vistas of
   self-potential.   **63, 69, 95, 96**
   Transform your walls into a
   bridge to help you transcend
   adversity and reach spectacular
   vistas of self-potential.

11. Leverage sweat equity built up by surviving previous trouble to help master current adversity.   **64, 67, 71**
95–96

Leverage your past experiences to reinforce your confidence in confronting your current problem.

12. Adversity always grants a chance to creatively resolve the problem.   **71**

Once you've been creative and come up with your solution, it's time to be innovative. Throw your ideas against the wall and see what sticks, remembering that there's no such thing as a mistake if you learn something from your actions.

13. Running away never helps.   **79**

Geographical cures change external circumstances, but the interior roads of motivation and emotion remain unexplored.

14. Overcoming adversity requires the right attitude . . . meditation . . . communication . . . and sharing.   **86**

These physical and emotional disciplines can help you become more familiar with the practice of loving yourself and others—a prerequisite for mastering the power of adversity.

19. Get perspective through acts of charity to others.

Giving can truly be the most *self*-ish act of all, because of generosity's tempering process and the simple fact that nothing makes you feel better than to give.

20. Adversity provides the only real opportunity to make an incredible difference in your life and in the world.

Before you right now is the opportunity to put your problems in perspective and thus transform your world—as well as *the* world—by giving of yourself to others.

21. Come to see problem solving as one of the great joys of life.

Embracing your adversity points to your greater purpose and connects you with a grander plan.

22. There is always a great idea lurking in adversity . . . Will you find it?

Continue to grow by taking advantage of all the new opportunities presented to you by your own, personal unending stream—and infinite bounty—of adversity.

APPENDIX B

Adversity Work Sheet

I. IDENTIFYING YOUR ADVERSITY

Use this section to identify your adversity and how you plan to master its latent power to improve your life using this book's tips and techniques.

1. What are the key facts about your adversity?

My adversity is that . . .

_____

_____

_____

_____

_____

2. What is your greatest problem concerning your adversity?

Due to my adversity, I am or feel . . .

_____

_____

_____

_____

3. What is your greatest fear concerning your adversity?

I'm frightened/worried/concerned that because of my adversity . . .

_____

_____

_____

_____

4. What are your goals concerning your adversity?

I would like to resolve my adversity so that I . . .

_____

_____

5. What past adversity can you leverage as sweat equity in confronting and mastering your current adversity?

Past adversity has helped to prepare me for mastering this adversity by . . .

_____

_____

_____

_____

6. What is your plan for resolving your adversity?

I propose to resolve my adversity by/through . . .

Positive thinking: _____

_____

_____

_____

Getting the facts about my adversity: _____

_____

_____

Being *self*-ish via acts of kindness in daily activities:

_____

_____

_____

Meditation: _____

_____

_____

_____

Communicative intimacy: _____

_____

_____

_____

Charitable acts of time and/or money to gain perspec-

tive on my adversity: _____

_____

_____

Using time wisely: _____

_____

_____

_____

II. TACKLING YOUR ADVERSITY

In this section detail evidence, experiences, and out-comes that support that you have followed through on your plan to resolve your adversities. Conversely, list here any problems you may have encountered in trying to implement your stratagems.

(Fill in all that apply.)

Positive thinking: _____

_____

_____

_____

_____

Getting the facts about my adversity:_____

_____

_____

Being *self*-ish via acts of kindness in daily activities:

_____

_____

_____

Meditation: _____

_____

_____

_____

Communicative intimacy: _____

_____

_____

_____

Charitable acts of time and/or money to gain perspec-

tive on my adversity: _____

_____

_____

_____

Using time wisely: _____

_____

_____

_____

III. RESULTS OF MASTERING YOUR ADVERSITY

In this final section, delineate and contemplate the benefits you have reaped through your attempt to master your adversity. Conversely, detail any obstacles/problems concerning your adversity that remain for you to master.

1. What progress/lack of progress have you experienced regarding aspects of your adversity?

(Fill in all that apply.)
I have seen progress in . . . _____

_____

_____

_____

I have *not* seen progress in . . . _____

_____

_____

(If there are aspects in which you have not seen progress,)
I intend to adjust/change my plan by . . .

_____

_____

_____

2. What sweat equity have you earned by mastering this adversity?

Mastering this adversity has prepared me for future adversity by/because . . .

_____

_____

_____

3. How has the experience of mastering your adversity affected you?

My adversity has tempered me, making me stronger in mind/body/spirit, by/because/through . . .

_____

_____

_____

Endnotes

1. Harold S. Kushner, *When Bad Things Happen to Good People* (New York: Avon Books, 1981), 59–60.

2. Tri Thong Dang, *Beyond the Known: The Ultimate Goal of the Martial Arts* (Rutland, Vt.: Tuttle, 1993), 88.

3. Thich Nhat Hanh, *Peace Is Every Step: The Path of Mindfulness in Everyday Life* (New York: Bantam, 1992), 58–59.

4. Yamamoto Tsunetomo, *Hagakure: The Book of the Samurai* (New York: Kodansha, 1983), 38.

5. Leslie D. Weatherhead, sometime minister of the famous City Temple in London, has inspired thousands all over the world with his spiritual conviction and faith. His noteworthy preaching is matched by his success as a writer, counselor, and psychologist. As the author of more than thirty books, Dr. Weatherhead has restated the truths of Christianity in a way that appeals to modern man.

6. Leslie Weatherhead, *The Significance of Silence* (New York: Abingdon Press, 1968), 41–43.

7. Hazelden Foundation, *Twenty-Four Hours a Day* (Center City, Minn.: Hazelden, 1954), 168.

8. William Shakespeare, *Hamlet,* in *Shakespeare Twenty-Three Plays and the Sonnets* (New York: Scribners, 1966), 706.

9. Norman Vincent Peale, *The Power of Positive Thinking* (New York: Prentice-Hall, 1956), 1.

10. Hazelden Foundation, *Twenty-Four Hours a Day* (Center City, Minn.: Hazelden, 1954), 197.

11. Jon Kabat-Zinn, *Wherever You Go, There You Are: Mindfulness Meditation in Everyday Life* (New York: Hyperion, 1994), 5.

12. Leslie D. Weatherhead, *When the Lamp Flickers* (Nashville, Tenn.: Abingdon Press, 1948), 91–94.

13. http://newtithing.org/content/richpoorgenerosityresearch.

14. http://marketplace.publicrado.org/shows/2006.

15. Arnold Bennett, *How to Live on 24 Hours a Day* (Hyattsville, Md.: Shambling Gate Press, 2000), 3–5.

Index

About the Authors

 **Albert J. Weatherhead** is chairman and CEO of Weatherhead Industries in Ohio, a private manufacturer of plastic closures for food, spice, pharmaceutical, and nutraceutical products. He has sixty years of experience in the plastics and metalworking industries and is the recipient of various U.S. and Canadian patents for metal-working processes and plastic products.

He is also the president of the Weatherhead Foundation; the founder of the Weatherhead East Asian Institute at Columbia University; founder of the Weatherhead Center for International Affairs at Harvard; founder of the Weatherhead PET Center for Preventing and Reversal of Heart Disease, University of Texas-Houston; and the founder of the Weatherhead School of Management, Case Western Reserve University.

Weatherhead is the author of *The New Age of Business* (Ohio University Press, 1956) and *John Parker Lindsay: A Study in Firepower* (American Society of Firearms Collectors Press, 1971).

He lives with his wife, Celia, in Ohio.

 **Fred Feldman** was an acquisitions editor at Dell and Fawcett before becoming a writer. He has published seventeen novels and coauthored three nonfiction works in the self-improvement and how-to business genres. An award-winning creative consultant, Feldman also travels the country advising Fortune 500 nonprofits on how to sharpen their marketing strategies and hone their donor communications. He lives in Massachusetts with his wife and daughter.

Advance Praise for
The Power of Adversity:

Among the Sufi's there is an adage: When you stand with your back to the sun your shadow is before you, but when you turn and face the sun your shadow falls behind. I met Al Weatherhead in 1994. Bright, accomplished, big presence, he was like daylight. Then, in an instant, darkness fell; he turned edgy, cool, and impervious. We all know these "turns" within ourselves. Faced intentionally and generously, these mind/heart shadows can become embers igniting an inner alchemical fire that cooks us into sustenance. Al describes in his unique voice and relentless honesty this alchemy. So doing, he details a practical path of mastery—of taking what is most difficult and using it to transform and be transformed into sunlight and nourishment for ourselves and the world.

Saki F. Santorelli, EdD, MA
Executive Director, Center for Mindfulness in
Medicine, Health Care, and Society;
Associate Professor of Medicine
University of Massachusetts Medical School

The Power of Adversity is packed with nuggets of wisdom.

—*Delos M. Cosgrove, MD,*
CEO and President,
Cleveland Clinic

Al Weatherhead's *Power of Adversity* has changed my response to daily bumps in the road and major catastrophic events. I will appreciate each challenge, and accept it as a gift to face my own shortcomings. So much of our suffering is the result of our own negativity. His wisdom helps me find solutions I never dreamed were possible.

—*Margaret Roche*
CEO, Stella Maris, Inc.

Hampton Roads Publishing Company

. . . for the evolving human spirit

HAMPTON ROADS PUBLISHING COMPANY publishes books
on a variety of subjects, including spirituality,
health, and other related topics.

For a copy of our latest trade catalog, call toll-free,
800-766-8009, or send your name and address to:

HAMPTON ROADS PUBLISHING COMPANY, INC.
1125 STONEY RIDGE ROAD • CHARLOTTESVILLE, VA 22902
e-mail: hrpc@hrpub.com • www.hrpub.com